MASTERING
the
MONEY MIND

MASTERING *the* MONEY MIND

A New Way of Thinking About Personal Finance

ED LAMBERT & ALEX CABOT

Mastering the Money Mind

A New Way of Thinking About Personal Finance

ISBN 978-1-5445-3053-6 Hardcover
978-1-5445-2993-6 Paperback
978-1-5445-2994-3 Ebook

For our children:

Avery and Elena Lambert and Samantha and Jack Cabot.

You have the gift of time. Use it well,

and keep making us proud.

CONTENTS

DISCLAIMER

The information contained in this book does not purport to be a complete description of the securities, markets, or developments referred to in this material. The information has been obtained from sources considered to be reliable, but we do not guarantee that the foregoing material is accurate or complete. Any information is not a complete summary or statement of all available data necessary for making an investment decision and does not constitute a recommendation. Any opinions of the chapter authors are those of the chapter author and not necessarily those of RJFS or Raymond James. Expressions of opinion are as of the initial book publishing date and are subject to change without notice.

Raymond James Financial Services, Inc. is not responsible for the consequences of any particular transaction or investment decision based on the content of this book. All financial, retirement, and estate planning should be individualized as each person's situation is unique. This information is not intended as a solicitation or an offer to buy or sell any security referred to herein. Keep in mind that there is no assurance that our recommendations or strategies will ultimately be successful or profitable nor protect against a loss. There may also be the potential for missed growth opportunities that may occur after the sale of an investment. Recommendations, specific investments, or strategies discussed may not be suitable for all investors. Past performance may not be indicative of future results. You should discuss any tax or legal matters with the appropriate professional. Diversification and asset allocation do not ensure a profit or protect against a loss. Rebalancing a non-retirement account could be a taxable event that may increase your tax liability.

Keep in mind that individuals cannot invest directly in any index, and index performance does not include transaction costs or other fees, which will affect actual investment performance. Individual investor's results will vary. The Dow Jones Industrial Average, commonly known as "The Dow," is an index representing thirty stocks of companies maintained and reviewed by the editors of *The Wall Street Journal.*

INTRODUCTION

"A person is smart. People are dumb, panicky, dangerous animals, and you know it."

—Kay, *Men in Black*

Tommy Lee Jones's character, Kay, wasn't talking about money when he said it, but he might as well have been. The truth is, an otherwise rational person can become their own worst enemy when it comes to their financial decisions, either by following their own primal impulses or by giving in to a mob mentality.

We've seen it a thousand times. Human beings are skittish animals, and their behavior shifts dramatically with their circumstances. In good times, they actively seek risky behavior. In bad times, they start heading for the hills. This behavior can lead to inconsistent and occasionally calamitous thinking when it comes to money.

It's all too common for someone with a well-designed investment portfolio to flush the whole thing suddenly in response to some traumatic event. An otherwise intelligent person who has been making careful investment decisions toward a long-range goal gets spooked by news reports about a market downturn, or they lose their job, or a close family member dies unexpectedly. The trauma becomes psychological justification for making a wildly irrational financial decision.

Consider the case of the hard-working engineer who suddenly lost his job after twenty-five years. Shocked, he thought, "Well, maybe this is a sign that I'm supposed to sell off all of my investments, buy a catamaran, retire early, and sail down to Aruba, even though I can't quite afford it." In doing so, he derailed a smart investment strategy and torpedoed his future.

People tend to overreact to bad circumstances. That's just human nature. It often happens because they receive poor advice, get spooked by alarmist talk from the media, or see other people making irrational decisions and blindly follow them.

Sometimes, it's not fear driven. Plenty of people use consumption to fill emotional holes in their lives. "I need a bigger house, another car, another expensive trip, a bigger wardrobe. Then I'll be happy."

Others go to the opposite extreme. "I can't spend a dime because something bad might happen to me down the road, so I'd better live like a miser." That's how you get millionaires living in ratty shacks, clipping coupons while the house slowly falls down around them. You know the type. Neighbors assume they're paupers, but when they finally pass away, the community is shocked to discover they were worth millions. What's the use of millions if you live a miserable life?

Irrationality tends to aim for the extremes, but rational thinking strikes a healthy balance, working toward long-term goals without making the short term miserable. With the right advice and a healthy perspective, we can all strike that balance.

THE DANGERS OF THE PRIMAL BRAIN

Unfortunately, our own evolutionary tendencies are working against us. Neurologically, we're programmed to deal with threats just like our tree-dwelling ancestors: lash out at the threat or flee from it. When something happens that seems potentially harmful, we will always revert back to that primal response. This tendency is fine if you're getting charged by a hungry bear in the woods. With a direct physical threat, "fight or flight" is the proper response nine times out of ten.

When it comes to financial decisions, however, "fight or flight" usually leads to trouble. Our primal brain has enabled us to survive and propagate the species for millions of years, but it isn't good for spending, saving, or investing.

To make smart long-term financial decisions, you sometimes have to act contrary to your primal brain. It's not an easy thing to do, and if you lack the knowledge or perspective to achieve your goals, it's going to be practically impossible. Couple this primal reaction with the all-pervasive mob mentality that afflicts the human race, and you've got a real recipe for disaster.

"Oh, wow, I keep seeing news reports about the market plunging a few hundred points," you think. "The pundits seem really freaked out! I guess I'd better sell my investments, take the money, and run!"

In modern society, we have multiple group dynamics influencing our decisions. Think about it. People are part of all kinds of identity groups: political parties, social clubs, online forums, social media, religious organizations, families, friend groups—so many opportunities for a mob mentality to override rational decision-making.

Alex conducted a little experiment at a dinner party once. A large group had come together at a restaurant. After the meal, the waiter approached and said, "Would any of you care for coffee?" For a couple of seconds, no one responded. Then a few shook their heads, a few others shrugged.

The waiter was just about to walk away when Alex said, "You know, I'd love a cup of black coffee. I have a long drive ahead of me."

Suddenly, seven or eight other people around the table spoke up.

"I think I'd like a coffee, too."

"Yes, that does sound good. Bring me a cup."

"I changed my mind. I want a coffee, please."

When it comes to an after-dinner coffee, that kind of mob mentality is not a big deal. When it comes to financial decisions, it can be a huge problem. It's dangerous to go with the flow unless you have a good reason for doing so.

If you could just step outside of your primal brain, away from the mob mentality, and even your own sometimes-irrational tendencies and desires, you would be able to make objective decisions about things like 1) the amount of money you spend, 2) the amount of money you invest, and 3) how and where you invest that money so it serves your long-term needs and objectives.

Put more simply, money should serve you rather than you serving your money.

SLICING THE PIE

People sometimes think of investment strategies as a simple game of finding what yields the best return, but the truth is it's first and foremost a psychological exercise. It's less about deciding if you should put your money in, say, a Roth IRA than it is breaking down your preconceived notions, prejudices, primal responses, and mob mentality to make reasonable and rational investment decisions.

Ultimately, there are four things you can do with your income:

- You can buy *things*.
- You can buy *experiences*.

- You can *save* money for some future consumption.

- You can *help* others.

View this as a pie cut into four slices. Consider how big each of those pieces should be, according to your own goals. This differs for each of us. You may put more money into experiences, like traveling the world, while your neighbor puts more into things, like buying a second home.

Ideally, you slice the pie in a way that you think is best for you. For example, if you really want to retire and leave the workforce early, you'll want to reserve more of your income for that future consumption slice. It's delayed gratification to achieve a cherished goal.

The point is your money is serving you, not the other way around. Slice the pie according to what you want to get out of life.

In Ancient Greece, people would go to the Oracle of Delphi when they needed guidance or understanding. Inscribed upon the pediment of the temple was the saying, "Know yourself." There are a few different ways to interpret that saying, but we think the most relevant is this: to determine the right course of action, you have to understand yourself and your own motivations.

What drives you? What scares you? What are your hopes and dreams? If you know all of these, then you're in a much better position to make the right decisions on your own. You won't need the Oracle of Delphi to tell you the correct path. You might benefit from a bit of gentle redirection, but if you know yourself, then you can make the right decisions about your future based on what you're trying to achieve.

That's what we do when we meet with clients seeking financial consultation. We're not there to tell them what to do. We're there to help them figure out what they want and provide the best options for achieving it.

Some people are very well-informed about their money but they make poor emotional decisions. Others can govern their emotions well, but they don't understand the fundamentals of investing. Still others are good at both but don't have the time to manage their own investments. Our mission as financial advisors is to have deep-dive conversations that help them get to the heart of what they really want their money to do for them, so we can steer them in the right direction.

That's our goal with this book as well.

In fact, we've been doing this for quite a few years. We came to the financial industry by very different paths, and from very different backgrounds, but we're united by the same core values and a singular mission.

A MINDSET MISSION: ED'S STORY

Ed first became fascinated with the stock market during the tech boom of the late nineties. He decided to study economics in college, and the more he learned, the more he realized, "There are a lot of people who could use some help with their personal finances." And so, by the time he was nineteen, he knew he wanted to provide financial advice for a living.

It proved to be an interesting time. Ed entered the industry in the spring of 2000 as an intern with Morgan Stanley, just a few short months after the tech bubble burst. For a while, many people misunderstood what was happening with the tech market. As a result, they made poorly informed, emotional decisions about their investments. It was an eye-opening experience for Ed, as he realized just how much more important it is to have good financial advice during challenging times.

He went to work for Morgan Stanley full time in 2001, where he eventually met and joined forces with Alex. His desire to help people with their finances became a true passion, and he's spent the last twenty years doing just that. Along the way, he's guided clients through some of the most challenging times: 9/11, the 2008 Great Recession, the COVID pandemic, along with a number of other challenging market environments in the past two decades.

With every crisis, he has only become more convinced of the importance of good financial advice. This conviction led him to the founding of Birch Run Financial in 2012 with Alex. It also led to the writing of this book, a continuation of his mission to help people make smart financial decisions that will enable them to achieve their goals in life.

A LONG ROAD TO A GOOD PURPOSE: ALEX'S STORY

While Ed knew that he wanted to be a financial advisor at the age of nineteen, Alex initially planned to become a physician. It wasn't until his sophomore year in college that he realized he wasn't interested in that line of work. Briefly, he considered joining the US Navy as a fighter pilot. He even took his physical exam and went through all of the tests.

But then he met the woman who would become his wife, and he realized he didn't want to head off to the Navy. He considered law school, but that didn't seem like the right choice either. He spent a year floating around, working for a time as a contract teacher at a Pennsylvania school.

After earning his licenses at A.G. Edwards, he came across a job opening at Morgan Stanley in 2008 that seemed like a good fit. Alex knew a lot about the markets because he'd read about them and taken economics classes. Also, he was good with numbers, and he knew he was good with people as well.

Growing up as the child of a single parent who worked all the time, he found himself accompanying his mother on countless business trips. At one time, they were flying to Washington, DC, every other week, and Alex was dragged to many business dinners, where he interacted with a variety of adults. He learned how to have conversations easily and keep people entertained and amused.

It seemed like his natural affinity and skills for interacting with people might be a good fit for the financial planning industry.

That eventually led him to Morgan Stanley in 2008, where Ed and Alex first met and joined forces.

THE JOURNEY BEGINS

Everything clicked as soon as we began working together at Morgan Stanley. While we have very different personalities and senses of humor, we are driven by a singular purpose: to help people develop a good financial mindset for long-term success that will enable them to achieve their personalized goals.

In the fall of 2012, we started our own independent company, Birch Run Financial, and we've been helping clients ever since. And that brings us to the book you're holding in your hands right now. This book isn't intended to answer every financial question you might have. Rather, its purpose is to help *you* start asking *yourself* the right questions so you can develop a good financial mindset and understand how to put your money to work for you to achieve the lifestyle you dream of.

We'll start by helping you understand just exactly what money *is*.

Chapter One

. . . .

WHAT IS MONEY REALLY?

It's a running joke in Alex's family that they don't really understand what he does for a living. He has tried to explain it, of course. We do retirement planning, we manage assets for clients, and we help them deal with financial challenges. Still, there has always been a lingering sense of ambiguity.

Whenever people ask his wife what he does for a living, she usually responds, "Ah, it's something to do with money."

Recently, Alex's young son approached him, held up a dollar bill, and said, "I don't understand why this piece of paper is worth anything. What is it?"

And being somewhat pedantic, Alex replied, "Well, son, it's not just paper. It's a blend of cotton and linen designed to be durable." The joke went right over his son's head, but Alex proceeded to explain the concept of currency. "That dollar represents more than just a number. It's a store of value that can be used as a means of allocating or saving capital. Let's suppose you had a hundred dollars right now. What could you do with that money?"

His son's eyes lit up. "Oh, I could buy a bunch of Lego sets," he said excitedly. He's obsessed with Legos at the moment so it was the first thing that popped into his head.

"What else could you do with it?" Alex asked.

"Well, we could use it to go out and buy dinner at a nice restaurant," his son replied.

"That's right," Alex said. "What else?"

"I guess I could give it to you, and you could invest it, because you're a good investor. Then it would become a whole bunch more money!"

"Yes, that's true," Alex said. "And there's one more thing you could do with that money. Do you know what it is?"

His son thought for a moment and finally said, "Maybe we could give it to someone who needed it. Like someone in our family who's having trouble."

"Exactly," Alex said. "We already have enough for ourselves, so we could spare some money to help someone in need."

Without realizing it, Alex's young son had given a fairly comprehensive overview of exactly what money can do. To put it as simply as possible, currency was invented in Mesopotamia about five thousand years ago as a way to replace the complicated barter system. It served as a way to store the value of labor, services, or physical commodities so that people could then trade that value for what they wanted.

In the ancient world, if you were really good at growing corn, you could grow enough to feed not only your own family, but others as well. You could grind it and store it, but it would only last for a finite period of time.

Instead, you could trade some of that corn to someone else in exchange for something. If that person raised cattle, they could trade you a cow for, say, ten bushels of corn. That was the fundamental principle behind the barter system: find someone who has what you want and trade them something they want in exchange.

The later innovation of currency as a medium of exchange allowed people to save and store value in an agreed-upon object of worth, rather than making a straight trade of goods or services. So instead of trading ten bushels of corn for a cow, you could sell your corn for so many units of currency. That currency stores the value of your corn. It's a bit like storing up potential energy that you can use to do other things.

Maybe you didn't need a cow right then, but the following month, you needed flour. Because you stored the value of your corn by selling it for currency, you were able to use that stored value to buy flour when you needed it.

That's the essence of money. It's a fascinating and fairly bizarre concept, and it evolved over time into greater levels of complexity. Eventually, the banking system came into play, and then, during the late Middle Ages, people started using gold as a deposit to enable them to purchase things on credit. This enabled banks to expand, and that, in turn, created our entire economic system.

However, it all goes back to the same basic human needs. With money, you can store value, which gives you the freedom and flexibility to use that value when you want to. And that, ultimately, is what money represents: freedom and flexibility. Put another way, money gives people choices in life.

A KID IN A CANDY SHOP

Imagine you're a kid in a candy shop. You've got a dollar in your pocket. What can you buy with it? Sadly, in 2022, not much. However, what if you have five dollars? Now you can select a couple of chocolate bars, maybe some gumdrops, or a big lollipop. The fancy stuff behind the counter is still out of your reach. No, you can't have the artisanal Belgian chocolate drizzled with raspberry glaze. It's beyond your purchasing capacity.

But what if we sent you into the candy store with fifty dollars? Suddenly, you have the capacity to buy just about anything you want, including that Belgian chocolate. It might be overpriced, but the experience of eating that Belgian chocolate seems very attractive to you. Of course, you'll also have a big dental bill in about six months when you pay to fill all of those cavities, but that's another issue.

You don't *have* to spend your fifty dollars in the candy shop. Maybe you just want to buy a single plain chocolate bar for two bucks and save the rest of your money for some other purchase later. Or maybe you're just a really nice kid, and you want to give some of that money to your little sister so she can buy some candy as well.

The point is a very basic one: when you have more money, you have more options.

Then again, with more options come more potential pitfalls. You could spend all of that fifty dollars on gumdrops. Since gumdrops are only ten cents apiece, you'd wind up with a big bag of them, but is that a smart decision? Are you really going to enjoy eating a gallon of gumdrops? Just because you have the purchasing power doesn't mean it's the right decision for you. That's something you have to figure out.

What if you walk into the candy store to find that it's jam-packed with people—all clamoring for the gumdrops. You ask someone why, and she replies, "Are you serious? These gumdrops are *incredible*. They're *amazing*. Everyone loves them!" Suddenly, even though you didn't walk in there intending to buy gumdrops, you find yourself considering them.

Let's complicate the issue. You're diabetic, and the gumdrops aren't sugar free. Everyone says you *have to try them*, they're affordable, but they're really bad for you. Suddenly, even though you have the purchasing power, and even though everyone else is doing it, the purchase is a very bad idea for you.

DON'T DWELL IN THE PAST

The amount of money you have directly influences the number of choices you can make: what neighborhood you live in, how many kids you can afford to have, what schools they can go to, what kind of vehicle you can drive, the vacations you take, and so on. Of course, the ultimate freedom is complete independence from a working income. Early in most people's careers, this is neither a priority nor an expectation. However, when you reach retirement age, it becomes a necessity.

Somehow, during your retirement, you have to generate enough income to live without needing to work. Doing that requires some amount of delayed gratification.

Unfortunately, we meet with many clients who have wasted numerous opportunities over the years to put away money for the future, and now that they are closing in on retirement, money controls their lives. Purchasing decisions they made years ago are determining their present *and* their future.

But as we always tell them, it's never too late to change the trajectory of your financial future, no matter how many bad decisions you've made in the past. Remember the old saying,

"The best time to plant a tree was twenty years ago, but the second-best time to plant a tree is today."

We never chastise people for making financial mistakes in the past. There's no benefit to dwelling on poor decisions you made with your money ten or twenty years ago, and nothing good comes from lamenting, "Oh, I wish I hadn't done that." You can't do anything to alter the past. All you can do is start making good financial decisions today.

This is important because sometimes people feel like they have to make up for the mistakes of their past. They make big financial changes in order to compensate for bad decisions in the past, such as investing aggressively on hot stocks to get as much return as possible.

"If I can get 800 percent return on this volatile stock, I'll catch up to where I should have been! I'll recoup all of those losses from my past!"

That's a very dangerous strategy that often leads to calamity. You can't play catch-up with the financial mistakes of your past. Indeed, it's rarely a good idea to look back at all. Instead, the best thing you can do is to say, "Here is what I have *now*. Here is where I'm trying to go. How can I get there?"

Forget the past. Look at the present and plan for the future. That's it. That's all you can do. The good news is anyone can do that, no matter what lies in their past.

Yes, if you'd started planning for your retirement in 2011 and invested all of your money in a single explosive stock like Tesla, you would be in a very good spot right now. But trying to do that is not much different than taking all of your money to Atlantic City and betting it all on black at the roulette wheel. There's a chance you might double your money, but there's also a chance you'll lose it all. That's the type of risk people sometimes take when they're trying to play catch-up for their past financial mistakes.

The prudent principles that govern sound long-term financial planning don't change just because of things you did years ago. Yes, as they say, "Gambling is the only addiction where you might wake up with $10,000 on your nightstand," but you're more likely to wake up with nothing. Don't gamble with your financial future by making wild, risky decisions to try to make up for lost time.

It might be too late to meet some of your original long-term financial goals, but there's nothing you can do about that. You might have to choose some different goals or tone down your expectations. Your conception of retirement might have to change from what it was twenty years ago, but you can still turn things around without being reckless. We know this from experience, and we've helped many clients accomplish it.

So, forget the past. Start today. To do that, we first need to figure out what you want.

Chapter Two

. . . .

WHAT DO YOU *REALLY* WANT?

Imagine someone offered you a million dollars with just one stipulation: you have to spend it all in one place. You can't spread it out. You can't allocate it to different things. It all has to be spent in one place.

What would you spend it on? Think about it for a moment. You have options. As we mentioned in the Introduction, you can boil those options down to four essential ways in which you can spend your money:

- You can buy material *things*.

- You can buy *experiences.*
- You can *save* money for future consumption.
- You can help *others.*

Maybe you'll spend your million on a thing. The possibilities run the gamut from the sensible to the completely frivolous. How about a million-dollar home? Or a million-dollar diamond-encrusted watch? You could even buy your own airplane, if that appeals to you.

Or maybe you'll spend money on some experience. These also run the gamut from the reasonable to the absurd. You could book a lavish whirlwind tour of temples of Kyoto, Japan, or you could charter a private yacht to sail around the world. If you have a health condition, you might pay for a very expensive experimental surgery.

But maybe you prefer to use that million dollars to help other people, in which case you could select your favorite charity and give them the entire lump sum. Then again, you could create an endowment for an organization that could spin off income for your charitable cause indefinitely. Or, if you know some people in need, you might give the money to them.

Finally, you can take that million dollars and put it all into some investment. Maybe you buy an equity fund, or you might decide to invest it all into some highly speculative investment. Or you might just stick it into a money market fund that's only going to earn very little and not even keep pace with inflation.

So, think carefully now. What would you do with that million dollars?

Here's the secret: there's not a single right answer. There's not one way to spend that money and "win." It all depends on what you want to achieve in life.

MAKING YOUR TRADE-OFFS

In reality, you don't have to spend all of your money in one place.

Unless you're Jeff Bezos or Bill Gates, you have limited resources, so you have to consciously decide how you're going to divide your money among the four categories.

Let's suppose you have about $10,000 a month to spend after taxes. The decisions you make about how you spend it requires trade-offs among the categories. If you spend $20,000 this year on a vacation, that leaves you with about $8,300 each month for other things. But what if you were to cut your vacation expense to $10,000 a year instead and invest the rest of it?

If you're forty-five years old and you start investing $10,000 a year at a hypothetical (but reasonable) rate of 6 percent per year, you'd wind up with $230,000 in fifteen years when you reach retirement. The question you have to ask yourself is, "Do I want to spend that extra $10,000 a year on vacations, or would I rather have $230,000 more for retirement in fifteen years?"

These are the kinds of conversations you need to have with yourself. If you don't thoughtfully break down your limited resources among the four categories, you're not going to optimize your money for your future goals. And it's not just money that's limited. Time is limited as well. To reach your long-term financial goals, you have to get your money to perform optimally for you in a limited amount of time, and that requires determining for yourself what you really want in life.

Do you want to retire early? If so, how badly do you want it? You'll have to put more of the limited resources toward saving for the future, which will require cutting out some of the things, experiences, and charitable giving that you might otherwise do along the way. Only you can decide how badly you want to retire early, which will translate into how much you allot for savings. If you prefer to retire at a traditional age, you can put less toward the future and spend more now.

Only you can decide what's most important to you. Would you rather own a larger house, a more expensive car, send your children to private school, or would you prefer to put more of that money toward retirement?

At the very beginning of your financial planning process, you need to sit down and figure out what you want to do with your limited resources. What is most authentic for you is going to differ from what's authentic to someone else. The point is to be intentional about how you allocate your funds among the four categories—things, experiences, helping others, saving for the future—so that you use them optimally to achieve your own long-term goals (not someone else's).

DO YOU NEED IT OR MERELY DESIRE IT?

As you consider the four ways you can allocate your resources—things, experiences, helping others, and saving for the future—break them down further into the *necessary* and the merely *desirable*. You *need* a roof over your head. You *need* some way to get to work. You *need* clothing and food. You *desire* a better car or a larger home or an expensive vacation.

Give priority to your needs over your desires in all categories. This too will be unique to you and your situation. A desire for you might be a need for someone else, and vice versa. For example, some people really do need at least one vacation a year for their own emotional and psychological well-being, but others can work the whole year without taking any time off.

Charitable giving generally has less of a need attached to it, but it may be something that you value very highly as part of your identity or lifestyle. For example, maybe you belong to a church that requires tithing, or maybe you are very cause-driven because of a personal experience or beliefs.

Regarding saving, you might have a certain amount that you *need* to save in order to live in the future, and a large amount that you *desire* to save in order to have a better lifestyle.

Once you've identified what belongs in each of the four categories, take some time to identify whether those things are needs or desires. Your needs give you a starting point. That's where you should begin allocating your limited resources. Whatever is left over can then be allocated to desires within the same bucket.

Let's say that your monthly income is $8,000. After all of your needs are taken care of, you have $4,000 left over. Now you can evaluate your desires and determine where to allocate that remaining income in each category.

You may find that your desires in each category exceed your remaining budget. If that happens, you can decide which desires to prioritize and which to leave unfulfilled. They're not necessary to your life.

We can represent this as a decision tree.

- At the top of the tree, you decide what belongs in each of the four categories (things, experiences, giving, saving).

- Then you decide which of these things in each category are *needs.*

- Then you decide which of these things are *desires.*

We recommend creating a decision tree like this for yourself. Write it down. Make something visual, because that will help you wrap your head around it.

It's a relatively simple process if you're willing to commit a bit of time and energy, and in the end, you'll have a clear picture of what you want to achieve and how you want your money to work for you.

DO IT ON PURPOSE

It's incredibly important to do this intentionally because it's unlikely that you will optimize your resources through chance, instinct, or emotion. This isn't simply a trick to maximize your investment portfolio. It's about becoming consciously aware of the choices you have with your money, and making those choices *on purpose* so they aren't made for you.

Sometimes, when we meet with a client for the first time, they will bring a huge amount of information about things like what they have in the bank, what they have in their 401(k) and investments accounts, pension accumulation, their budget. But when we talk about what they're trying to accomplish in retirement, they have only a haphazard, slipshod idea.

To use our previous example, let's suppose the client has an income of $8,000 a month. They know they have about $4,000 left over after paying for all of their needs, but they don't really know what to do with that money. They don't have many desires, except that they don't want to spend all of the money or go into debt. Beyond that, they don't really know what they want. They've never really thought about it.

Other clients come to us, and we learn that they spend a huge amount of money on vacations, or they drive really fancy cars, or they have some other expensive hobby, but the money is spent without any self-examination. They might look at their budget and say, "Oh, I have a thousand dollars left over at the end of the month. I could afford a really big car payment, and I'd kind of like a nice car today."

It's not a purchasing decision flowing out of preset objectives, just an emotional decision made in the moment. In both instances, we suggest that people first examine what they really want in life. What are their long-term objectives? What are they working toward?

To use an example that hits close to home, Alex's mother would absolutely love to go to Fashion Week in Milan. She has mentioned this to him a number of times, and he has always said, "You have the financial resources for it, Mom. Why don't you just go?" But each time, her response is the same: "It seems like such a frivolous thing to do."

There's nothing wrong with doing something that seems frivolous if you're passionate about it *and* you can make it work. If you have the resources, and it won't adversely affect the rest of your life, set the objective and go for it! Just make sure you're doing it intentionally and you have the financial capacity and resources for it.

Remember, you're trying to clarify *your* needs, wants, and wishes. You're trying to set *your* goals, not someone else's. Be very careful that you're not comparing yourself to others and trying to live someone else's ideal life rather than your own. "Keeping up with the Joneses" is a marketer's trick for making us think the wrong things are important, but it's a lot harder to avoid than we think it is.

Next, we'll look at how you can avoid making unhelpful comparisons when setting your goals.

Chapter Three

AVOID COMPARISON

The neighborhood where Alex lives is a quiet, middle-class, suburban neighborhood with about sixty homes and a lot of families. It's a pleasant place to live. Most of the people there would be considered upwardly mobile, reasonably successful, with an average household income of at least $150,000 a year. In other words, they're successful and comfortable, but they're not multimillionaires.

Over the years, Alex has observed a rather bizarre phenomenon in his neighborhood. Anytime one person does some kind of outside renovation on their property, others will soon follow suit. If one house puts in a new deck, within six months there will be construction vehicles all over the place as more people put in new decks.

When Alex first moved into the area, only one house had a swimming pool. Now, there are quite a few, and one massive stone pool surrounded by statues and a giant slide that doesn't quite match the decor of the rest of the neighborhood. When one neighbor bought a Jaguar SUV, soon other Jaguar SUVs began to appear in driveways and garages.

That's the way the neighborhood operates. Everyone is trying to keep up with the Joneses. Pools get installed and rarely used. Unusual cars get purchased and rarely driven. New decks get put in and then neglected. All because people are constantly comparing themselves with their neighbors.

Another wave that swept through the neighborhood was stone patios. Alex's next-door neighbor put in a beautiful stone patio with a fireplace and a nice walkway that led to the deck. It was a beautiful and idyllic outdoor setting. Within months, other stone patios were being installed along the street.

Alex's home was one of them. But here's the difference. Alex and his wife spent a lot of time at his next-door neighbor's house, and they loved hanging out on that patio. They knew if they installed one in their own home it would get a lot of use, and they loved the idea of creating an outdoor living space where they could enjoy the neighborhood when the weather was nice.

So, after a few years and some intentional discussion, they had a stone patio installed. They made the space unique, customizing the layout to their own needs and wants, and they've gotten a lot of enjoyment out of it. The difference is that they weren't simply latching onto a fad because it seemed like the thing to do. They measured it against their own wants and made a decision accordingly.

CONSUMED BY CONSUMPTION

What we see in Alex's neighborhood, we see in society generally. People tend to spend money in ways they think they're *supposed* to spend money. They follow the examples set by others and try to fulfill expectations imposed by society.

That's why when someone gets a raise and starts making more money, they increase their cost of living, even if they don't need to.

"I'm making more money now. I guess I should buy a really nice car. That's what people do at this income level, right?"

Technically, they're better off, but are they happier? According to a study conducted by Princeton University in 2010, a person's day-to-day happiness increases with their income up to about $75,000 at which point it tops out. While more recent studies have contradicted that finding, one thing is sure: if you're spending money on things that do not fulfill either your wants or your needs, then you're wasting your precious resources.

Unfortunately, it happens all of the time. People compare themselves to others and make financial decisions accordingly. We live in a consumption-driven society. Much of the spending is discretionary; as a result, many people become hyperconsumers and wind up without the financial security that they could have built for themselves.

When we discuss the timing of retirement with clients, one of the questions that often comes up is whether or not it will be a problem if they decide to work a few more years beyond their planned retirement date. We always tell them, "Very rarely." In fact, the only time we've seen this hurt a client's retirement is when they take a different job and start making a lot more money.

For example, a client earning $150,000 might sit down and create a retirement plan predicated on the idea of continuing that $150,000-a-year lifestyle throughout their retirement years. They set that goal and work toward it. Then, a year or two before retirement, they take another position that pays $300,000, and it changes their lifestyle. It also resets their financial expectations.

"Oh, this is how we're supposed to live during retirement, isn't it?"

Now, they really want to continue living their new $300,000-a-year lifestyle, but they've only planned for half of that. They haven't been saving and investing for a $300,000-a-year lifestyle, and there's really not enough time left to adjust their retirement plan that dramatically, but they are strongly tempted to try.

The "Joneses" they're trying to keep up with in this instance are their own changing expectations. This is sometimes referred to as *lifestyle inflation.*

So the danger isn't just about comparing yourself to your neighbors, friends, family, coworkers, or random people on social media. It's also about comparing your own desires to your income level. If your income suddenly spikes near your retirement date, it can create a disconnect in your own mind: "I was happy in my $150,000-a-year lifestyle, but now I'm making

$300,000 and living a more expensive lifestyle. Shouldn't I keep it up during retirement?"

In the book *The Millionaire Next Door*, authors Thomas Stanley and William Danko revealed the results of their long study of wealthy people across numerous occupations and industries. They discovered that certain occupations are full of hyper-consumers who tend to do a lot of high-end discretionary spending relative to their income. Many of these individuals have big houses and expensive cars but relatively low net worth.

In other industries, the reverse tends to be true: people have relatively high levels of net worth compared to their income.

What drives the hyper-consumerism in certain industries? Peer group expectations. People expect their peers to have very nice things: a nice car, a nice house, a nice watch, a nice suit, and so on. "Everyone else in the company owns a half-million-dollar home and drives a BMW, so I suppose I should as well."

In other occupations, people don't have the same expectations about their peers. Nobody says, for example, "Oh, he's a civil engineer like me. Why is he driving such an old car? Why doesn't he wear a designer watch? What kind of shabby engineer is he?"

The peer group expectations of our coworkers place a huge set of expectations upon us, whether we realize it or not. As the old saying goes, "If you have to tell people you're smart, then you're probably not smart." We might also say, "If you have to tell people you're rich, then you might not be rich."

It reminds us of a picture we've seen floating around the internet of Bill Gates and Warren Buffett standing together at a conference. If you didn't know anything about them, you would assume they were just two regular, slightly awkward guys. They're dressed very plainly and have messy hair. They kind of look like Midwestern dads. The caption above the picture reads, "$162 billion in one photo and not a Gucci belt in sight."

Obviously, these two men are extremely wealthy beyond the capacity of most people who have ever lived, but they feel no obligation to flaunt that wealth. They don't need to prove to their peer group or anyone else that they're rich. Now, to be fair, Bill Gates owns a collection of classic Porsches and a gigantic yacht. He's not just sitting on his wealth. He practices some big-time conspicuous consumption based on his own interests, but he doesn't do it to keep up with anyone. He didn't wake up one morning and say, "Gosh, I'd better buy a fleet of Porsches so I look as successful as all of the other Silicon Valley CEOs!"

You don't have to prove anything to anyone—not even yourself. Don't follow the crowd, and don't try to keep up with the Joneses. Spending money to make people think you're rich will only end up making you poor. You don't get rich writing a bunch of checks! You obtain financial freedom through smart and intentional decision-making.

WHO'S AFRAID OF A LITTLE FOMO?

While Ed was in college in the late nineties, he often overheard guys in the local gym locker room sharing stock tips with each other. It was the heyday of the tech bubble, when excessive speculation in dot-com startups led to a period of massive growth in stock prices, and these guys loved to share the most ridiculous investment advice with each other, most of it about internet-related stocks.

They weren't experts or full-time investors, but they were always worked up about the ridiculous possibilities. As we all know, the tech bubble burst in 2000, and all of the bad advice people followed came back to bite them.

We see it with every bubble. During the tech bubble, it was all about investing in highly speculative tech stocks. During the housing crisis in 2008, it was all about leveraging money to buy properties. Most recently, it's all about cryptocurrencies and meme stocks. In each instance, people are driven by a phenomenon called FOMO (fear of missing out), and they end up making some woefully ill-advised investment decisions because "everyone else is doing it."

Investment FOMO causes people to stray from well-thought-out investment plans into the realm of pure speculation. A lot of people with good portfolios in the late nineties, getting great returns, just couldn't resist the siren call of even more massive returns from speculative companies like Copper Mountain, JDS Uniphase, and Lucent—many of which no longer exist.

So let us put it as eloquently as we can: who gives a rip what other people think? You're going to be so much better off in your own financial life if you don't care about your peer group, neighbors, or social media influencers.

A couple of years ago, Ed was at the hospital as his wife was giving birth to their second daughter. He accompanied his mother-in-law down to the parking garage, but she couldn't remember exactly where she'd parked. As they wandered the levels looking for her car, they came across a section of the garage that was chock-full of expensive luxury vehicles.

If not for the fact that the parking garage was attached to the hospital, Ed might have assumed it was a parking area for Fortune 500 CEOs. In reality, it turned out to be the area reserved for doctors. The median income for a physician in the US is about $243,000,[1] and some of these cars cost more than that. Spending more than a year's salary on a vehicle just to park it in a garage most of the day—it just doesn't seem like a smart financial decision.

At the same time, the fact that every car in the doctors' section of the parking garage was of comparable quality and expense provides us with a stark example of the power of peer group expectations. Can you imagine how it would feel to be the lone physician parking his Honda Accord in that sea of Mercedes, Porsches, and Bentleys?

Yet, if it's not a big priority for you to drive a Mercedes, driving a much more affordable car that meets your needs is just about the smartest thing you can do. That gives you more financial resources you can spend on the things you really do need or want, or on a better retirement lifestyle.

---

[1] "Average Doctor Salaries by Specialty," Kaplan Online, accessed January 16, 2022, https://www.kaptest.com/study/mcat/doctor-salaries-by-specialty/.

So what's the best way to avoid being driven by these kinds of comparisons with other people? Obviously, you can't help but notice when every house in your neighborhood installs a big stone patio. If you're a doctor on your first day on the job, you can't help but notice that every other doctor drives a super-expensive car to work.

To some extent, we're going to see what other people are doing with their resources. This is why it's so important for you to stop and clarify exactly what *your* needs and wants are. Think about the lifestyle that *you* want to have outside of the judgment of any other person. Yes, that big-time Instagram influencer posted photos of herself in a private jet, and it looks amazing. The neighbor down the street installed a giant swimming pool surrounded by marble statues, and it's impressive. But what do *you* really want for yourself and your family?

Take some time to do some real deep self-reflection. Are you investing in something because it means something to you and your family, or are you simply checking off a box on a list of expectations based on your profession, industry, neighborhood, or something else?

It doesn't make sense to install a swimming pool if your family doesn't enjoy swimming. It doesn't make sense to drop a bunch of money on an expensive car if cars don't mean much to you. Whenever you see conspicuous consumption on the part of other people, consider carefully if it's something you would truly derive pleasure from. If not, don't buy it! Never use your money just to fulfill the expectations placed upon you by other people.

In doing so, you might miss out on some really nice things in life that *do* matter to you and your family, and wouldn't that be a shame? Use your financial resources in a way that makes sense for you and your family, whether anyone else gets it or not.

Alex really loves Italian and German supercars, and he would love to own a Ferrari. However, he has two young children, and one of them is still in a booster seat. The astronomical cost of a Ferrari notwithstanding, he knows it's not practical, so he does not give in to that temptation.

Only you can look at yourself in the mirror and make the right decisions for your financial future based on your own needs and wants. Don't let anyone else do it for you!

Chapter Four

. . . .

DEFINE YOUR FINANCIAL FREEDOM

Here's the key question: what does financial freedom look like for you? How clearly can you define it? For example, Ed loves his job, and he thrives in his career, so financial freedom for him would mean being able to do his job for free. If he had enough money that he didn't need the income generated from his work, he would still gladly provide financial advice to people without charge. He loves it that much.

Alex, on the other hand, loves to travel, so financial freedom for him would be the ability to travel all over the world whenever he wants. His ideal retirement would involve retiring to Scottsdale, Arizona, joining a nice country club so he could play golf when he wanted to, and frequently traveling to places he's never been before. And like Ed, he would continue to provide financial advice along the way because he enjoys helping people.

Your idea of financial freedom doesn't have to look like anyone else's. It just needs to be authentic to you. For many people, financial freedom would mean never having to get up in the morning and going to work. For most, it means being able to spend money on what they want. If they want to fly to Europe next week, they can. If they want to take a cruise to Japan, they can.

Of course, you don't have to stop working to be financially free. As Mark Twain allegedly said, "If you love your job, you'll never work a day in your life." So there's no harm in continuing to do some work in retirement if you derive pleasure and a sense of fulfillment from it.

In every case, however, financial freedom boils down to one thing, and this is the common denominator for everyone: not having to worry about money. That's the point we all long to get to, isn't it? What we do beyond that point will vary wildly from person to person. Many would go straight to their boss the moment they achieved it and quit on the spot. If that's how you feel, you're certainly not alone. As comedian Drew Carey put it, "Oh, you don't like your job? There's a support group for that. It's called everyone, and we meet at the bar."

With financial freedom, you can do what you want. You can work. You can *not* work. You can travel. You can buy things. You can play golf every day. For some people, not much would change. For others, it would be a radical transformation.

What would it be for you?

WHAT ARE YOU RUNNING TOWARD?

In our experience, we've found that most people don't have explicit financial goals, or they have them but don't work toward them consistently. They have an income. If they're lucky, they might have a pension—though pensions have become quite rare. They might have a 401(k) plan and a little put aside in savings. However, there are no specific goals, and furthermore, they're not sure what the money they have today will mean for them at sixty-five.

They know what they're worth, but they can't answer questions like, "If I continue to spend, save, and invest at my current pace, how much income will I have at sixty-five? And how will that contribute to my financial freedom in retirement?"

As Lewis Carroll wrote in *Alice's Adventures in Wonderland*, "If you don't know where you're going, any road will get you there."

Consider your own situation. Do you have any idea what kind of lifestyle your money today can provide for you at retirement? More than that, do you know what you want to work toward?

If you're not sure, then we strongly encourage you to spend some time setting retirement goals. Think carefully about what you want to work toward. Realistically, how long do you want to maintain your current occupation in your current position, and what do you want your retirement lifestyle to be? Sit down and outline this.

Make sure your goals are SMART: Specific, Measurable, Achievable, Relevant, and Time-bound. We've provided a short template at the end of this chapter, which outlines SMART goals, guidance, and space for you to add your own goals. We recommend selecting three specific things you want to achieve in the short term, medium term, and long term.

Once you've set some explicit goals, look at what your money is doing for you right now. How much are you saving, and what's the expected return on that money? How much money are you likely to have when you reach your goal date?

Let's suppose you want to stop working in ten years. Is it a pipe dream? If you work twelve years instead of ten, will it make that pipe dream possible? You might not be saving enough money to meet your objective. How much more do you need to put away?

These are the kinds of questions you need to clarify. Most people haven't done that. They're a bit wishy-washy about what they want for the future, and they're just meandering through their financial lives. When we talk to clients, we sometimes have to break the news to them that their goal isn't possible at their current pace, especially when they come to us just a few years before retirement.

By age sixty, the die has already been cast for some people because there was no thoughtful planning about their financial future. They might not be able to produce enough money to reach their goal, in which case the goal will have to be adjusted.

One of the most common questions we hear from people is, "How much money do I need to retire?" The answer is always,

"You need as much as you need." In other words, it depends on your retirement goals and the lifestyle you want to live. That's why it's so very important to clarify your retirement goals up front.

There's a strategy some younger people have started to embrace called FIRE, which stands for "Financial Independence, Retire Early." The idea is to save and invest aggressively in early adulthood in order to retire in your thirties or forties. To do this, you have to live frugally, spend very little, and avoid big expenses before then. That means sharing an apartment with others, not having kids, and putting as much money as possible into a dividend-producing investment or some other kind of diversified portfolio.

Ideally, by the time they reach thirty-five, they can live off the modest distribution rate of their investments for the rest of their lives. There are risks to this strategy, but at least the people who embrace it have a very defined goal. They know what they want, and they have a clear destination in mind, so they can sit down and figure out how to get there with their financial resources.

We can't emphasize this strongly enough. *Set your retirement goals. Clarify what you want to achieve.* Just remember, circumstances can change, and so can your desires.

For example, a twenty-two-year-old just out of college who wants to be completely financially free at thirty-five probably can decide to live a rather austere lifestyle. They're used to living in a dorm or small apartment, eating cafeteria food, and they're probably not married. They haven't had many life experiences yet. However, their outlook on life might change quite a bit by the time they reach thirty-five. They might get to thirty-five and realize, "If I retire now, I'll be living the same meager lifestyle I had at twenty-two. I think I'd rather get married, raise kids, buy a nice home, and travel a bit. I probably need to work a little longer and set a goal farther down the road."

Similarly, you don't know what the economy or markets will be like at retirement. Even if you set a goal and create a solid plan to reach it, you might have to pivot and make adjustments to your plan along the way. Be willing to do so.

Having a bad financial plan is just as ineffective as having no plan, and an *inflexible* plan that is never revisited is a bad plan. Set your goals, work toward them, but be flexible.

Clarify Your Personal Financial Goals

1) Identify three specific things you want to achieve in the short term, medium term, and long term.
2) Make sure each of them is SMART: Specific, Measurable, Achievable, Relevant, and Time-bound.
3) Write them down.
4) Reevaluate them periodically over time.

START WITH THE END IN MIND

Always start by defining your retirement goals. In a sense, you are setting the long-term goal first and working backward from there to create a path to reach it.

Where do you have to be in five years in order to get closer to your long-term goal? Where do you have to be in one year? Don't just think through this in your head. Sit down and write it on paper. Set your goals and revisit them over time so you can make necessary adjustments.

Once your goals are set, determine what actions you're going to have to take to achieve them. Will you need to *make* more money? Will you need a promotion? Do you need to leave your current job? Do you need to *set aside* more money? If so, how much?

This is what we mean by setting the destination and working backward to determine a path for getting there. Set SMART goals and make adjustments along the way. In fact, when you're working on your budget or writing your financial plan objectives, we recommend using a pencil instead of a pen. You'll probably use a computer, but the point remains the same. Be flexible and realize that changes will come. You might have to adjust your financial goals or objectives along the way.

For example, you might get laid off and struggle for a while to find a comparable position. That changes your financial trajectory, so you will have to adjust your expectations. Conversely, you might plan to retire in five years, but before that happens you get a massive promotion. Now you're making more money and finding more fulfillment in your job. Maybe you change your goal so you can keep working for ten more years.

Ultimately, there's no shortcut to reaching a long-term goal. You're playing a long game here, so play it well. Let's look at how you can do that next.

SMART GOALS WORKSHEET		
Specific	Who is involved? What do I want to achieve? When do I need to achieve this? Why is the goal important?	
Measurable	How will I measure my progress? How will I know if my goal is achieved?	
Attainable	Will it be clear when the goal is complete? Is it reasonable to complete the goal in the allotted time?	
Realistic	Is the goal related to my overall success?	
Time-bound	How long should it be to accomplish this goal? When will I check in on if the goal is complete? Am I ready to start work on the goal?	

Chapter Five

....

PLAY THE LONG GAME

Alex grew up as an only child in a single-parent household, so he spent a lot of time alone, reading or watching television. His mother worked long hours, but every night they would sit together in their little townhouse in Convent Station, New Jersey, and watch *World News Tonight with Peter Jennings* on ABC.

Around age eight, he started paying attention to the news more intently, and every night, Jennings would talk about the performance of the Dow Jones Industrial Average. Of course, Alex didn't know what the stock market was. He asked his mother about it, but she was a physician, not a financial advisor.

She explained as best she could by saying, "There are companies that people put their money into, and the Dow Jones is a group of those companies. When the number goes up, it means people are making money. When the number goes down, it means they're losing money." A very simplistic explanation, but Alex's eight-year-old mind could understand it.

Then the big stock market crash of 1987 came along, and the Dow Jones lost 20 percent in a single day—the largest single-day percentage decline in the index's history at that time. People were panicking, and there was a lot of talk on the news about what investors should do. Alex has vivid memories of the fear and uncertainty being expressed in the media.

On Friday nights, his mother would pick him up from school at 5:30 and take him to Short Hills Mall, a big shopping mall in an affluent part of North Jersey. They'd eat dinner at a restaurant called Baker's Garden, then walk around the mall and window shop. As a kid, Alex loved it, and one of his favorite activities was to throw pennies into the mall fountain and make a wish. On the Friday after the stock market crash, he went to the mall as usual with his mother. When he came to the fountain, his mother gave him a penny, and he knew right away what he wanted to wish for. Clutching the penny in his hand, he thought, "I wish the Dow Jones Industrial Average would get to three thousand points!" And then he tossed his penny into the water.

GROWTH IS INEVITABLE BUT IT'S A LONG GAME

It might seem like a strange thing for an eight-year-old to wish for, especially when he had no investments of his own. You know what's even crazier? The fact that the Dow Jones Industrial Average is now well over 30,000. Think about how much the market has grown since the late eighties. Despite the stock market crash of '87, Desert Storm in 1991, the tech bubble burst in 2000, the September 11 attacks in 2001, the Great Recession in 2008, and the COVID crash in 2020, the market is worth vastly more today than it was in Alex's childhood.

Consider the fact that the stock market got cut in half *twice* during that period of time: from 2000 to 2003, when the tech bubble burst, and from 2007 to 2009, during the recession. Despite the perennial bad news, all of the market downturns, recessions, and setbacks, the stock market has still massively increased its value over the long term.

This is undeniable, so why don't people *feel* like the market is going to produce those big returns? Why do so many people *feel* like the market is constantly on the verge of losing massive value permanently and unrecoverably?

The answer, of course, is that people focus on the day-to-day fluctuations of the stock market, and it makes them feel like there's no way to make money.

The world population is growing, we're developing new technology, and we're becoming more productive and efficient, so you can trust that growth is going to happen. Even if there are setbacks along the way, growth is almost certainly going to happen! Stock market growth isn't always steady. It won't happen every year, but unless capitalism as we know it ceases to exist completely, you can rely on growth in the long term.

Ed started working at Morgan Stanley right before 9/11, and he can still vividly recall a chart in the conference room that showed the long-term growth of the US stock market from 1920 to the present day. At that time, the market was struggling to recover from the tech bubble bursting, and the consistent long-term growth over eighty years was reassuring.

Then 9/11 happened. In one week, the Dow Jones dropped from nearly 10,000 to almost 8,000. During those difficult days, Ed would sometimes look at that chart and think, "I hope the long-term growth bears out again. Otherwise, we're in trouble." The magnitude of the turmoil seemed different this time. Worse than ever. Maybe the market wouldn't recover this time.

Of course, with time, we've seen the stock market do exactly what it has done after every downturn. It eventually recovered and more! Just before 9/11, the Dow Jones was at 10,000, and at the time of this writing, it has more than tripled to 35,000. Faith in the long-term growth of the stock market has been rewarded time and time again. The long game works.

The nineties was the heyday of day traders who were all trying hard to get rich overnight by making big bets on dot-com stocks. These days, we still see people trying to make fast money on all kinds of speculative bubbles. It's a "win the lottery" mentality that leads to excessive risk taking, and most people who attempt it get wiped out.

There is just no free lunch in the investment world. If a stock produces higher than market rate return, it's because people perceive it to be riskier and more volatile.

Look at the performance of some of the highest-flying stocks in the last few years: Tesla, Facebook, Netflix, Amazon. The rate of return on these has been insane. Of course, we all wish we'd stuck all of our money into them. The problem is, for every high-flying stock like Amazon, there are plenty of companies that grew like crazy at one time then lost all of their value and went bankrupt. People just tend not to remember them.

This is called *survivorship bias*, the tendency to emphasize the performance of existing stocks and overlook the ones that have gone bust. We look back and think, "If only I had gotten in early to Amazon, Facebook, Tesla." It seems like it'll be easy to pick the next Amazon stock and make big money in a short period of time.

You might get it right, but you're more likely to get it wrong. Either way, when you seek a much-higher-than-average rate of return, you expose yourself to a lot more risk and put your portfolio in danger. So, what's the answer?

Personally, we view our own portfolios as relatively conservative, even though nearly all of our investments are in the stock market. Since we know we have at least twenty years before we need to touch any retirement money, we can broadly diversify across thousands of individual stocks. We're not exposed to the volatility of any single company. While we're not getting the big returns from any high-flying stocks, we are getting the returns that the market as a whole delivers.

We're not trying to pick the right stock. We're not investing in something that will grow 50 percent in the next six months because we know we'd have an equal chance of losing 50 percent or more in that same period of time. It's not a risk we're willing to take. We're playing the long game, so we're betting on the consistent, long-term growth of the stock market as a whole—a bet that has paid off time and time again throughout the history of the United States.

Think about it. If you invest $100,000 at a 6 percent rate of return, that money is going to be $200,000 in twelve years, $400,000 in twenty-four years. You have quadrupled the value in twenty-four years with only a modest 6 percent rate of return.

When the return compounds on itself, it produces a snowball effect. As Albert Einstein allegedly said, "Compound interest is the eighth wonder of the world. He who understands it, earns it... he who doesn't pays it." Want to play the long game well? Invest in assets that produce a reasonable rate of return that compounds upon itself over a long period of time. That's what we're doing in our investment portfolios, and that's what has consistently paid off since the stock market began.

So the first year, you make 6 percent growth on $100,000. You end up with $106,000. The second year, you make 6 percent growth on $106,000, and you end up with $112,360. The third year, it's $119,101. Then $126,247. And so on. In other words, the pace of your growth increases each year because you're earning 6 percent on an increasingly larger sum of money. It's a snowball effect that builds up speed over time. You're not just earning 6 percent of $100,000 over thirty years, you're earning 6 percent each year on a larger and larger sum of money. That's the power of compound interest, and after thirty years, it can transform a modest rate of return into amazing growth.

Most people want to be successful, but they don't see the power of playing the long game when it comes to investments. When someone retires with a lot of money, other people see the end result, but not all of the consistent hard work that went into achieving it.

A kid fresh out of college will look at a successful fifty-year-old and marvel at the trappings of their success, but they don't see the decades of work that went into it. The Porsche, the big house, the nice clothing—it's all the result of years of hard work. This is true in almost any profession. An athlete who makes millions in a pro league got to that point after years of honing their craft through high school, college, and possibly minor leagues. They spent a long time playing hard without making a penny for it before they were offered a big contract.

Just because you come out of college with a respectable degree doesn't mean you're instantly going to make big bucks. You have to start low in your industry and work your way up the ladder over ten to twenty years before you really reap the rewards and get a high-paying position. That's how the real world works. You don't graduate from college and immediately become the vice president of a large financial firm. As the old saying goes, "The only job where you start off at the top is digging a hole."

When you graduate and get a job that feels beneath you, it's not beneath you. While you may possess knowledge and ability beyond what you're doing, you're not yet worth a lot to your company or potential clients. It's going to take time to acquire that value.

The starting salaries of physicians are very high, but a starting physician has spent years in medical school, followed by internship and residency. It's a long road to a high salary. It takes time and experience to get to the top and make big bucks. In terms of your career, to achieve long-term success, you hang in there, work hard, learn more, build a reputation, and make progress one rung of the ladder at a time.

As Ray Kroc, the CEO who franchised McDonald's restaurant, wrote in *Grinding It Out: The Making of McDonald's,* "I was an overnight success all right, but thirty years is a long, long night." Kroc transformed McDonald's from a single burger joint in San Bernardino, California, to a massive global enterprise. He is one of the most successful entrepreneurs of all time, but it took him thirty years of hard work to get there. For years, he was slogging away selling Prince Castle milkshake machines out of the back of his car.

Similarly, it takes a long time to become an expert at anything. Think about how many hours of practice and study are required to master the violin. According to Malcolm Gladwell, it takes about ten thousand hours to master anything.

The same holds true for generating real, consistent wealth for retirement. Chasing fast money with volatile investments is more likely to be a losing game than a winning game, but trusting the long-term growth of the market has worked without fail.

A LONG CLIMB TO THE TOP

Real financial success usually takes a long time and a lot of patient hard work as you let compound interest do its work on your investments. At the same time, growth is not linear, even if it inevitably trends upward. The 136-year history of the Dow Jones Industrial Average is pockmarked by setbacks, some of which we've already mentioned in this chapter, but the long-term results have been tremendous. We've bounced back—and then some—from every single setback. That's the key! And unless the whole world economic system collapses in a global apocalypse, the overall growth of the market will almost certainly continue.

Therefore, if you want to reap the rewards, you need the resilience to deal with those setbacks. It won't do you much good to get pumped up about compound interest if you dump your investments the second you see a slight downturn in the stock market. That's like going through medical school, internship, and residency, finally becoming a physician, only to quit after your very first surgery doesn't go the way you wanted.

Setbacks are going to happen, so be ready to deal with them. In his basement, Alex has one of those electronic basketball hoops that you see in video game arcades. His kids love playing it, and sometimes he joins in. Though he's not a great basketball player by any means, he can defeat a twelve-year-old and an eight-year-old with ease.

On one occasion, when his son was upset about losing by a single three-point shot right at the buzzer, Alex asked him,

"Hey, son, who do you think has missed more basketball shots in his lifetime: me or Michael Jordan?"

His son instantly said, "You, of course, Dad! Michael Jordan is one of the best basketball players of all time."

And Alex replied, "Nope, Michael Jordan has missed *way* more shots than me."

"How is that possible?" his son asked.

"Because he's *taken* way more shots than me," Alex explained. "I've never played professional basketball. I played a little bit in grade school, and I play this arcade machine with my son, but Michael Jordan learned and played the sport competitively for most of his life. He took hundreds of thousands of shots, and some of them missed. But over the course of his career, despite missing plenty of shots, he racked up a ton of wins and became a legend in the sport."

And that, folks, is kind of what financial success looks like.

Chapter Six

. . . .

SETBACKS WILL HAPPEN

When asked about his outlook on the stock market, financier J.P. Morgan always gave the same three-word answer: "It will fluctuate."

In fact, there are two things we can say about the stock market with relative certainty. First, that it will continue to grow, and second, that it will continue to fluctuate.

It's a bit like driving. If you hop in your car and drive down the street, it's statistically unlikely that you're going to run into a roadblock, detour, traffic jam, pothole, or have an accident.

However, if you drive across the country, then it's almost certain that you will run into at least a few of these along the way.

The farther you drive, the more likely it becomes that you will run into a few problems. The same goes for investing in the markets. The long-term results have historically been very good, but there have also been a number of major setbacks and downturns along the way.

If your investment strategy spans years, or decades, then you are inevitably going to encounter a few major setbacks on the road to long-term financial success. Thus, if you want to stay the course and achieve your objectives, you should prepare yourself both emotionally and strategically ahead of time to deal with them.

We've seen people making the same mistakes over and over again with their investments for the last twenty years, so when we talk to clients, we like to conduct what we call a "fire drill." We take them through a bunch of possible setbacks and discuss their responses. That way, they can avoid making the kinds of emotional mistakes with their investments that are so very common.

When taking a cross-country road trip, smart drivers hope for a safe trip, but they are emotionally and strategically prepared for flat tires, bad weather, road construction, and other possible problems. They've got insurance, a spare tire, maybe a AAA membership, and so on.

Alex recently returned from a national park tour with his wife and kids. They visited six national parks in ten days, which entailed putting two thousand miles on a nice rental car. Fortunately, they had a GPS service to guide them along the way, which helped them avoid wrong turns, heavy traffic, and highway construction. And whenever Alex missed a turn, the GPS rerouted him so he could still get to his destination by the shortest possible path.

While they were driving back from Mesa Verde National Park on their way to Zion National Park in Utah, severe storms swept into the area, and he had no choice but to drive through them. Fortunately, he knew they were coming, and he was emotionally prepared to deal with the intense rain. He slowed down and paid more careful attention to the road ahead.

At the same time, his wife looked up information about the storm and learned that there were extreme flooding and mud-slides happening at Zion National Park. They weren't supposed to arrive at Zion until the next day, but she got nervous. Alex and his wife began to discuss if they needed to change their plans.

"Should we turn back? Should we head to a different destination?"

As it turned out, by the time they got to Zion the next day, the storm was gone, and there was no flooding. They didn't have to change their plans at all, and they wound up at their planned destination without any difficulty.

It's very similar to what we see in the world of investing. You set a destination and make your way toward it. Even if your plan is well made and wisely guided, you will encounter some disappointments along the way, and you will hear about big potential risks down the road. There are going to be times when you wonder if it'll all come crashing down, and in those times, you might be tempted to make drastic changes to your financial plan that simply aren't necessary. Even if you have to occasionally slow down a little and pay more attention, you're still going to get to your destination.

THE IMPACT OF RISK AVERSION

The performance of the stock market speaks for itself. The market has risen in value thirty out of the last forty years. It lost money in ten of those years, which translates to a 25 percent loss rate. Over that same period of time, it produced a compounded rate of return of 8.9 percent. If you started with $100,000 forty years ago and accrued $10,000 a year, you would now have $6,317,285, even if you lost money 25 percent of the time.

Let that sink in. A proper investment strategy wins out every time. No matter how frequent or how severe the setbacks have been, the smart investors who held out over time during the last forty years have reaped a massive reward. And this is despite the fact that some of the setbacks during the last forty years have been *huge!*

Well-balanced portfolios have done well through multiple recessions, national tragedies, and an historic pandemic. The stock market has been cut in half twice, but the overall result has still been extremely positive.

Two psychologists, Daniel Kahneman and Amos Tversky, conducted a landmark study on loss aversion and discovered that people feel a financial loss twice as intensely as a financial gain. So the average person will feel as strongly about a 10 percent loss in value as they do about a 20 percent gain. That tendency makes people overly risk averse, and as a result, they fail to see the big picture and make short-term decisions that are counterproductive to their long-term plans.

To overcome this tendency, accept that setbacks are going to happen—both market and personal setbacks—and have some plan for dealing with them.

When dealing with a market decline, it's important to remember that, based on the overarching historical trend, the market will eventually recover. The stock market has fully recovered and more from every single bear market, crash, correction, pullback, downturn, recession, and plunge in the history of the market. Remind yourself of this simple historical fact: the market has *always* rebounded eventually.

As long as the economic engine of the world continues to turn, the market will always rebound sooner or later. Make financial decisions accordingly. Our natural inclination is to eliminate the cause of our anxiety, so when the market declines, we want to dump our investments and run. It's like putting your hand against a hot stove. Your brain tells you to quickly pull away.

It's not even a fully conscious decision, just a fight-or-flight response from the amygdala as your body senses a threat. Your muscles tense up, your breathing increases, your heart rate goes up, and your pupils dilate. This is an evolutionary response that we've developed against predators.

"Here comes a hungry beast. We'd better get this body in gear, so we can get out of here!"

Here's the problem: when it comes to economics, the markets, and financial planning, your primal instincts are dead wrong. All of that evolutionary programming is dead wrong. You can't react to a 20 percent market downturn the way your tree-dwelling ancestors dealt with a hungry saber-toothed tiger. "Fight or flight" are both wrong.

Flight usually means cashing out. Sometimes, people flee from a market downturn by moving all their money into an asset that has no potential for growth. "We'll park our assets on the sidelines until the danger passes," they say. This is counterproductive to your long-term financial plan.

Here's a scenario we've seen: Bob sees the market drop 20 percent, so he moves all of his investments to cash and dumps it in a non-interest-bearing account. Afterward, the market declines another 10 percent, and Bob feels like his prudence has been rewarded. "Oh, I made the right decision," he thinks. "Look at how much more I could have lost!"

But then the market recovers. It's back to the place it was when Bob got out, but he hesitates to get back in. His fear response was rewarded, so he's still hypersensitive to perceived volatility. Then the market grows beyond the point where he left it. Finally, Bob buys back in, except now he's missed out on some of the growth.

If he'd just stayed in the market, he would have enjoyed all of that market growth, and he wouldn't have lost a single penny—the threat that he ran from wasn't real!

This kind of behavior is why *most* individual investors underperform.

Generally speaking, humans make awful decisions about the timing of investments because our primal brains are constantly working against us. As financial advisors, a big part of what we do is coach people through these periods.

Anytime the market goes through a rough patch, clients call us and say, "What should we do now? What's the best way to react to this?" In almost every case, the answer is to rebalance and buy *more* stocks while they're down. Then just sit back and let the market bounce back—because it will!

If you can't stomach buying more stocks when the market is down, the least you can do is hold tight to your allocations and wait for the market to return on its own. It might take six months, it might take five years, but it has *always* rebounded. Will it always rebound in the future? We think so. Of course, we can't guarantee that in writing, but the historical trend is crystal clear.

That doesn't always matter when a client is panicking and desperately wants to stop the pain by selling out, but selling out will only stop the pain temporarily. The negative impact on your financial plan, on the other hand, might last a very long time, especially if you wait too long to buy back in and miss out on substantial growth.

Fortunately, we haven't had many clients bail on their allocations over the course of our careers, but we've dealt with countless people in the throes of panic mode. During a market problem, you might discover the hard way that your personal risk tolerance is lower than you originally thought. That's okay. Rather than moving everything to cash and parking it all to one side, just reduce your risk profile, create a more conservative portfolio, and you'll be protected from some of the market's volatility. We've done that for a few clients, and while it's not ideal—after all, you're still selling some of your securities at a lower price—it does help them avoid losing out on some of the growth that comes when the market rebounds.

HOW MUCH RISK CAN YOU HANDLE?

So, if you discover that you don't have the stomach for market setbacks and volatility, we recommend finding a happy medium where you adjust your risk profile and make some conservative changes rather than pulling out of the market completely. Dial your risk level down until the market recovers. You might still lose some of the market growth when it does, but you'll lose less of it. That way, you won't fall as far behind on your financial plan.

Just like it's okay to change lanes when you're driving somewhere if something up ahead is making you nervous, it's okay to adjust your risk profile in the middle of a financial plan. Slow down, use your turn signal, and make the lane change carefully, and you should be fine. You can move back into your original lane once you've passed the object in the road. Chances are, you will still get where you want to go.

What you don't want to do is suddenly jerk the steering wheel to the left and cross five lanes, because then you're likely to crash. And if you crash, you're definitely not going to reach your destination.

Shifting to a more conservative allocation requires some

negotiation, as you try to determine what is optimal for you. However, it's better than bailing out.

Your *financial* capacity for risk and your *psychological* capacity for risk might be very different from each other. While your finances can handle an aggressive allocation strategy, you may find that you can't handle it mentally or emotionally. Furthermore, you may find that your psychological capacity for risk changes depending on what's happening in the world.

Indeed, we saw people making very aggressive investment decisions in 2020 with Robinhood and other online trading apps to a degree not seen since the peak of day trading in the nineties. The financial capacity for risk didn't change, but the psychological capacity for risk changed for a lot of people because of what was going on in the world.

Sometimes, the greatest volatility we deal with is our own ever-changing emotional state. Keep this in mind as you make investment decisions. Avoid drastic changes, and you should be okay in the long run.

Long-term financial progress is never linear. Study the history of the markets, notice the various downturns along the way, and prepare yourself for future downturns mentally and emotionally. Build out your investment plan ahead of time and make sure it's designed to handle the unpredictability of the market—both good markets and bad, because you're going to encounter both.

A POTHOLE YOU CAN'T AVOID

What do you do before you set out on a long road trip? You input your destination on your GPS app and map out a route to get there. Then you take note of possible roadblocks, traffic problems, construction, and other hazards. Along the way, the GPS is going to reroute you sometimes in order to avoid problems, but you'll still arrive at your destination on time.

As financial advisors, we're a bit like that GPS app. We help people get to where they want to go, show them how to deal with problems along the way, and help them recognize when they need to reroute so they arrive at their destination safe and sound in the end.

There is, however, one pothole in the road that you can't completely avoid. It's in every lane of every road in front of you, and you're headed right for it no matter how fast or slow you're going. Changing lanes won't help. Changing routes won't help. That pothole is coming.

What is it?

Inflation.

The purchasing power of your money is eroding over time no matter what you do. As Milton Friedman said, "Inflation is taxation without legislation," and "Inflation is like alcoholism; the good effects come first." We'll see what you can do to avoid the effects of inflation next.

Chapter Seven

REFRAMING RISK

Many of our clients were alive during the seventies and experienced the super-high inflation that plagued that decade. They know what it looks like to see prices rising dramatically in a short period of time, and they understand from experience the impact that it makes on purchasing power. In more recent decades, inflation has been relatively low, so younger clients sometimes don't think about the impact it has over time.

Our monetary system is designed to have a few percentage points of inflation per year. That's how central banks control the money supply and interest rates. But inflation is a bit like high blood pressure—you may not notice it for many years, but eventually it causes serious systemic problems. A pile of money parked in a bank account gradually loses purchasing power over time.

If you don't invest your money in a way that earns at least as much as the inflation rate over time, then it will naturally erode. That's one reason (among many) why it's a bad idea to keep your money in bags in your closet.

Most people don't even think about this. Investors tend to focus on things that seem scary (but, historically speaking, aren't scary), like short-term market volatility, without realizing that the thing they should really be scared of is inflation. The markets have always recovered from volatility and gone on to new highs, but inflation just keeps chipping away at the value of your money over time—relentlessly, constantly, year after year.

We can think of this in medical terms. If market volatility is an acute condition, then inflation is a chronic condition. What's the difference? An acute condition is severe but temporary, like a sinus headache. It comes out of nowhere, and it's extremely painful. But you take some Advil, and in an hour or so, the headache goes away. That's how it is with market volatility. It's painful, it can come out of nowhere, but it soon passes.

Inflation, on the other hand, is like a chronic condition, a long-developing syndrome whose effects are increasingly felt over time. High blood pressure is a common chronic condition. You can't necessarily feel its effects in the moment, but over time it may be weakening the arterial wall of a blood vessel in your brain. If you don't do something about it, eventually that arterial wall is going to burst, and then you might die.

As with chronic conditions, you don't necessarily see the true impact of inflation on your money over the short term. Often, our clients are hyperaware of market volatility, but they don't notice how inflation is chipping away at their purchasing power day after day.

To truly see the long-term effect of inflation, you have to look back many years. A pound of hamburger meat that cost $4.04 in 2021 cost $3.99 in 2008. That's not a big enough difference to make much of an impact, but if you go all the way back to 1990, you find that a pound of hamburger meat was only $0.89. A gallon of gas that cost $2.87 in 2021 cost $2.05 in 2009, but an astounding $0.36 in 1970. Suddenly, the erosion of purchasing power becomes clear.

That's the slow, steady march of inflation. You don't see it, but it is constantly eating away at the value of your money.

Unfortunately, people tend to ignore the effects of inflation when making their financial plans. Sometimes, clients will say, "I would just like to keep my money in cash because then there's no risk of loss."

And we always reply, "If you keep your money in cash, we can 100 percent guarantee you that it will decline in value over time."

Yes, if you keep your money in cash or a non-interest-bearing checking account, there's no risk of loss from market volatility, but you're experiencing a constant decline in value from inflation. It's a very slow loss, so you might not notice it, but it is relentless. Every single year, that same pile of cash is worth a little less than the year before.

YOUR MONEY IS LEAKING

The main reason you invest money is to avoid losing purchasing power over time. Over the last twenty years, inflation has been about 2.2 percent. What does that mean in terms of purchasing power? It means if you'd parked $1 million in cash in a bag in your closet twenty years ago, it would only buy you the equivalent of $650,000 of stuff today. It's a guaranteed loss!

Just consider how prices have changed over the decades as a result of inflation.[2]

Average Cost of a New Home

2018: $385,880

2000: $119,600

1980: $68,700

1960: $12,700

Average Cost of a New Car

2018: $35,742

2000: $21,850

1980: $7,200

1960: $2,600

---

[2] "Comparison of Prices Over 90 Years," The People History, accessed January 4, 2022, https://www.thepeoplehistory.com/70yearsofpricechange.html.

Average Cost of a Loaf of Bread

2021: $2.12

2000: $1.26

1980: $0.50

1960: $0.22

If you're retiring in twenty years, the cost of everyday living is going to be a lot higher. Have you taken that into account in planning for your retirement?

Of course, some things have gotten more affordable over the years. Alex grew up in the mid- to late 1980s and attended a private school in a relatively affluent part of New Jersey. One of his richest friends owned a fifty-inch television, which was a big deal back in 1987. It cost a whopping $5,000, which is the equivalent of about $15,000 today. Then again, today, you could buy a fifty-inch television for $400.

When Ed went to college in the nineties, he bought a laptop for $2,100. Today, he could buy a laptop that's fifty times as powerful with a hundred times the memory for about $300.

Some aspects of our lives are cheaper today than they were years ago, chiefly technology, which can lure people into a false sense of security.

Inflation is very real, and your money doesn't go nearly as far today as it did thirty years ago. Yes, the computer or television you bought twenty years ago would be a whole lot cheaper now, but food, gasoline, vehicles, homes, clothing, and almost everything else has become drastically more expensive. The money that you parked in your non-interest-generating bank account has been leaking value year after year, and it will continue to do so, because that's how our monetary system works.

The only safe and prudent approach is to assume the cost of living will continue to rise, so you should be prepared for at least a modest compounded rate of inflation. Design some portion of your long-term investments to deal with it. Otherwise, your results are going to be very different from what you envisioned.

In the end, while short-term market volatility might be scary, it's not dangerous. On the other hand, inflation isn't scary, but it's extremely dangerous. In the next chapter, we'll introduce a way of thinking about your investment allocations that can help you deal with inevitable inflation—and a whole host of financial issues.

Chapter Eight

ASSET CLASSES AS "BUCKETS"

When an orchestra performs a symphony, every musician has a part to play, and every instrument contributes in its own way to create beautiful music. The various string instruments are doing one thing, the woodwinds another. If there are multiple instruments of the same kind, and one of them is missing, it's hard to tell, but if an entire section is missing, then the whole symphony sounds off.

You need brass, percussion, woodwinds, and strings, but you may not need every single instrument in every section. If you're missing a single flute, you can still create beautiful music. The end result might not be exactly what the composer intended, but it still sounds nice. As long as the broad categories are covered, you can get away with missing a few instruments.

On the other hand, if you have one instrument that is wildly out of tune, it's going to sour the whole symphony. If a single horn is blaring in the wrong key, it'll be very apparent that something is wrong. If a viola is playing the wrong song, it's going to stand out. If a clarinet is a half step off the beat, it'll be obvious in every bar of the symphony.

In many ways, your investment portfolio works the same way. Every investment is like an instrument in an orchestra, and ideally, each one is playing its role in harmony with the others to achieve your overall objectives. As long as you allocate the right way, broadly speaking, then you're okay, even if you don't have every little nuance just right.

Maybe all of your bonds aren't diversified properly, but as long as you have a good mix overall, the result will be roughly the same, even if it's not optimal. However, just like the instruments in the orchestra, if one asset class is completely off base, then you're not going to get the results you want. It will create a dissonance in your portfolio that moves you further from your goals.

In other words, even if you can't represent every single

"instrument" in your portfolio exactly the way it should be, you might still be able to create a reasonable approximation of the intended outcome, as long as all of the broad categories are represented and no single instrument is way out of tune.

It might also be helpful to think of your investment portfolio as a football team. Think about the offense on your team. You have a quarterback, running backs, tight ends, receivers, and linemen. Each offensive formation uses a different number of players in each position, but the broad categories must be covered. For example, no formation works without some number of linemen because they have to protect the quarterback.

If the Tampa Bay Buccaneers took the field with no linemen in their formation, Tom Brady would be on his way to the hospital within the first few minutes. You can change the number of linemen, but the broad category must be covered. Conversely, if a single lineman is playing completely wrong, it can blow up the whole offense.

If you watch football at all, then you've seen this happen. You've watched a game where the quarterback got sacked because of one weak link in the offensive line who couldn't make his block. It happens all the time. The exact number of linemen can change, but if one of your linemen doesn't hold the line, then the defense is getting through. Generally speaking, you don't have to pay attention to every single player on the field unless one of them really messes up.

GETTING YOUR BUCKETS IN ORDER

Similarly, every part of your portfolio is important and has a job to do. However, as long as your portfolio is well designed, and all of the broad categories are covered to achieve your objectives, then you don't have to obsess constantly over every single investment.

Typically, in a balanced portfolio, you will have certain investments that are designed for growth and periods of time when there's a lot of growth in the market. Other parts of your portfolio exist to absorb risk when things aren't going well, so you can withstand volatility. It can be helpful to think of these different parts of your portfolio as buckets into which you are tossing your assets.

In general, in any portfolio, you should have a growth bucket and a stable bucket. Your growth bucket is going to fluctuate a lot, but it can make you a lot of money. Your stable bucket won't fluctuate much and won't make you nearly as much money, but it will provide stability to the overall portfolio.

How much you put in each bucket will change depending on what the market is doing. Young and aggressive investors may put all of their money into stocks, and when the stock market declines, the whole portfolio will fluctuate. This is rarely the case for retirement planning. If you're at or near retirement, then you may want to design a portfolio that doesn't fluctuate as much.

As long as you have a significant percentage of your assets in that stable bucket, you can draw on it when the markets enter a period of volatility. This also provides a buffer if your psychological risk tolerance is low, as you're less likely to make a snap decision.

To be clear, we're not talking about segregating your accounts into an aggressive account and a conservative account. Instead, we're recommending a single portfolio with a variety of investments, using the bucket analogy to separate those investments into broad categories, some stable and some volatile, in order to create a well-balanced portfolio.

As we said, this mitigates the emotional response to volatility. Let's look at how it might work.

Let's suppose your portfolio is comprised of 50 percent stocks and 50 percent bonds. Stocks are going to follow the volatility of the market, but bonds are usually more stable.

With a 50/50 split, if your stocks drop 10 percent but your bonds stay flat, then your portfolio as a whole will be down 5 percent. In a $1 million portfolio, that means you're down $50,000. If you were wholly invested in stocks, then you would be down $100,000. There's a huge difference in the psychological impact of losing $50,000 or losing $100,000. For someone who can't stomach a big loss, this can mitigate just enough of the risk to keep them from making an emotional, reactive decision.

Look at your own long-term financial plan, estimated cash flow needs, and your assumption about your returns. Adjust how much you're putting into each bucket according to your own financial risk tolerance within a narrow range. Then tweak it higher or lower depending on your *psychological* risk tolerance.

It's a strategy we've used many times when markets fluctuate and clients get nervous. In the above example, a client would lose $50,000 out of their $1 million portfolio.

First, we encourage the client by reminding them that the

loss could have been $100,000. "You have $500,000 that's *not* invested in the stock market," we remind them.

Often, this is enough to help them hang in there until the market recovers. We brought many clients through this same struggle during the COVID crisis in 2020, because so many people were worried about how long it would take the stock market to recover. Remember, the market lost 34 percent in just over a month in 2020. That's enough to scare a lot of investors and send them packing.

"How long is it going to take the market to recover?" clients would ask. "Is it *ever* going to recover?"

We would remind them about their years of cash flow needs, and then point to the money in their stable bucket. "Look, your $500,000 in bonds hasn't been touched by the market decline. That's a big part of your portfolio, and you can spend that for years while you wait for the stock market to come back!"

Mitigating the psychological risk factor—that's the role your stable bucket plays in your investment portfolio. This is just as important as the linemen on a football team preventing the quarterback from being sacked, because the very worst thing you can do with your investment portfolio is bail out.

If you bail out, you lose money from the market downturn, you start losing money from inflation, and you miss out on growth when the market rebounds. Allocate between the buckets however you need to in order to alleviate your anxiety so you can deal with stock market volatility.

DISTRIBUTION DANGERS

Having said that, we'd like to respectfully disagree with a bucket strategy used by some of our fellow advisors for dealing with distributions after retirement. Once you retire, you're going to continue managing risk as you take money out of your portfolio to meet your cash flow needs. Some advisors recommend drawing those distributions from your stable bucket *first* and leaving your growth bucket alone for ten years or more. The idea is that you won't have to worry about market fluctuations for a large part of your retirement.

Here's the catch: if you draw solely from your stable bucket during the first decade of your retirement, then the amount of volatility in your portfolio will increase over time. Once the stable bucket is depleted, then your entire portfolio is comprised entirely of stocks, and now your whole portfolio is subject to volatility. If you haven't diversified and the stock market enters a dramatic downturn, then you're in for a wild and scary ride late in your retirement.

For that reason, we recommend looking at the totality of your allocation and determining where you are comfortable setting your risk tolerance. Don't shift to a more aggressive allocation if you can't handle it.

Take, for example, a fictional client named Kelly. She has $1 million in a growth bucket comprised of stocks and another $1 million in a fixed bucket comprised mostly of bonds. During retirement, she draws out $100,000 a year. Let's assume that she draws down her fixed bucket for the first ten years, then she shifts to drawing half from the stable bucket and half from the growth bucket.

After the first five years, two-thirds of her remaining money is in the growth bucket. After ten years, her stable bucket is gone, and all she has now are growth investments. Her whole portfolio is subject to market volatility, and her investment profile is a lot more aggressive than she ever wanted it to be.

Instead, we recommend periodically moving some money from your growth bucket into the stable bucket that you're drawing from so you're constantly rebalancing your portfolio. It's a bit like being a conductor in a symphony. Make sure all of the sections of your investment portfolio are balanced so the whole orchestra plays on throughout your retirement.

It's normal for one investment bucket to struggle. At any particular moment, there are going to be a few things in your portfolio that aren't doing particularly well, but that's not predictive of what's to come. Everything has its purpose, so don't make panicked, emotional, or spur-of-the-moment decisions in response to volatility.

Balance the assets in your investment buckets in a way that meets your psychological risk tolerance. That way you can take the primal brain out of your investment decisions and stick with a well-balanced plan that's going to meet your future cash flow needs.

Chapter Nine

HINDSIGHT IS 20/20

When it comes to investing, we always remember the winners that we missed, but we rarely think about the losers that we also missed.

"Oh, if only I'd invested in Google. If only I'd invested in Apple. If only I'd invested in Tesla. Think about how rich I would be now."

We think like this all of the time, don't we? We daydream about investments we should have made that would have brought about wild success. Shouldn't we also be thankful for all the failed companies we *didn't* invest in, especially the ones that everyone said were going to be winners?

Shouldn't we also say, "Oh, I'm so glad I didn't invest in Enron. I'm so glad I didn't invest in Pets.com?"

This is something we remind people about every time they see an individual stock break out and lament that they didn't invest a bunch of money in it. Yes, when you look at the performance of stocks over a period of time a handful will stand out as absolutely stellar performers, but for every stellar performer there are many stocks that have crashed and burned.

For every Amazon, there's a JDS Uniphase. For every Google, there's a Copper Mountain. For every Netflix, there's a Blockbuster Video. There have been countless stocks that everyone thought would do well that ultimately collapsed. When we mention them to clients, they often reply, "I've never heard of those companies. JDS Uniphase? Copper Mountain? Who are they?"

And, of course, that's the point. Many people have never heard of these companies because their price collapsed and, in many cases, they went bankrupt.

Why do we remember the winners and forget the losers? It's called *survivorship bias*, and it's our human tendency to view the successful performance of existing stocks as a representative sample without regarding those that have failed.

History is written by the winners, but when planning for our future, we run into trouble if we only look back at the ones who have succeeded greatly. The volatile stock that's fluctuating wildly right now might not be the next Tesla; it might be the next Enron.

For every success you failed to take advantage of, there are numerous failures that you managed to avoid. Why not pat yourself on the back for avoiding the failures, instead of cursing yourself for not investing in the big-time winners?

Even better, why look back on your investing past at all? You can't change the past anyway, and there's no guarantee that a past success story will be repeated in the future. The only thing you can do is look at today and plan for the future.

In this industry, we see predictions from analysts and market prognosticators constantly. They tend to speak boldly about what's going to happen. Sometimes those predictions come true, but more often than not, they're wrong. People always remember when they follow an analyst's advice and reap the reward, but they tend to forget when the analysts are wrong. If a so-called expert makes a hundred predictions and only five of them come true, people will remember the five that came true and forget the ninety-five that were way off base. This is just human nature.

In 1996, Alan Greenspan, then chairman of the Federal Reserve, warned investors in the tech sector about their irrational exuberance. Tech stocks were blowing up at the time and producing incredible returns, but he sounded the alarm that there wasn't much actual value behind the growth.

"Irrational exuberance has unduly escalated asset values, which then become subject to unexpected and prolonged contractions," he warned.[3]

As it turned out, Greenspan was dead right. The stocks were overvalued. The peak didn't come until early 2000, but when the bubble burst, it erased years of gains in tech stocks and wiped out billions of dollars in market capitalization.

People remember his speech about "irrational exuberance" now because he turned out to be right, but if someone had listened to his speech and immediately sold all of their stocks, they would have missed out on a pretty significant run from 1996 to 2000. And if you'd diversified your portfolio appropriately, balanced your investments properly between the buckets, then you would have been just fine, even when the tech bubble burst.

---

[3] Adam Hayes, "Irrational Exuberance," Investopedia, last modified August 4, 2021, https://www.investopedia.com/terms/i/irrationalexuberance.asp.

WHEN ANALYSTS ARE INSTIGATORS

In March 2009, at the absolute nadir of the financial crisis (the market bottomed out on March 9, 2009), a famous economist named Nouriel Roubini wrote an article in *The New York Times* declaring that the market still had about 15 percent to drop before it would become even remotely attractive to potential buyers.

He predicted that the recession would last a lot longer, and the fallout would be worse. That article was published on the very day that the market hit rock bottom. The S&P 500 was 676 on March 9, 2009.

If you'd read that article and made a snap decision to get out, then you would have missed the opportunity to rebalance at an optimal place, and even if you'd realized your mistake, you couldn't have gotten back into the market at the same price. From that point on, the market went up, and it's gone up ever since. It has never come close to the low it hit on March 9, 2009.

Sometimes, analysts get it right, sometimes they're right but their timing is off, and sometimes they're just completely wrong. As we said, everybody remembers Alan Greenspan's speech because he was right, though his timing was off by a few years. Very few people remember Nouriel Roubini because he was wrong.

That's why you have to be very careful getting guidance from the prognosticators. As the economist John Kenneth Galbraith put it, "The only function of economic forecasting is to make astrology look respectable."

Then again, hindsight does have its uses. For example, it can be valuable to look at past events and think about how they could have played out differently. That can help us make better decisions. For example, if you put all of your money into one stock and it doesn't perform well, it would be wise to look back and realize there's a good lesson to be learned from that. "Maybe I shouldn't put all of my money into one stock."

In that sense, hindsight can be valuable. It's important to take lessons from the past, but make sure you're drawing the *right* lessons from your experiences. As Bill Gates said, "Success is a lousy teacher. It seduces smart people into thinking they can't lose."

Here's how this plays out for some clients: "Wow, look at how

Tesla's stock performed! I should have gotten in early. Therefore, I'm going to bet big on some other tech startup because it might be the next Tesla."

That's a bad lesson to draw from the past, because you can't know who the next Tesla is going to be!

Imagine if you took $10,000 to a casino and bet it all on black at the roulette table. You have roughly a 45 percent chance of doubling your money on a single spin of the roulette wheel, so it's not the worst bet in the world.

The dealer spins the wheel, and it comes up black. You did it! You doubled your money. That's 100 percent return on investment with a single spin of the wheel.

Here's a question for you: was that a good investment?

Answer the question for yourself before you read on.

When we ask clients this question, there's always a prolonged pause. Of course, it seems like a good investment. You doubled your money with a single spin of the roulette wheel. Folks, that's survivorship bias at work. The only reason it seems like a good investment is because the wheel landed on the right color in the past. There's no guarantee that it will land on the right color the next time you make that bet.

In fact, statistically, it's a poor investment decision, because the house has a 5 percent advantage. That means for every $100 you bet, you're going to lose, on average, about $5 over time. Yes, in one instance, the results were spectacular, but over many repeated instances, it's going to work against you.

Betting everything on a single roulette color seems like a good decision now because it worked out for you in the past, but continuing to make the same bet over and over is going to hurt you.

This problem works in both directions. Sometimes, a smart investment doesn't work out the way you expected in the short term, so you assume it was the wrong investment to make.

"Boy, that was a stupid decision," you say. "I lost money on that investment. I shouldn't have done that."

You can analyze an investment, set the right level of risk tolerance, diversify your portfolio, make a reasonable decision, and it still might not work out for you in the short term. That doesn't mean it was the wrong decision. Given the information you had at the time, along with your objectives and level of risk tolerance, you made the best possible decision at the time, but it was affected by something beyond your control. Just because it didn't work out the way you hoped doesn't mean it was the wrong decision.

Ideally, we're making decisions based on rational analysis, not gut feelings and emotion, but even then, some smart investments won't perform as well as they should. That doesn't mean we shouldn't make similar rational investment decisions in the future, because over the long run, reasonable decisions based on analysis are going to work in your favor.

Yes, you've failed to invest in some winners over the years, but you've also failed to invest in some big-time losers. Stick with the fundamentals, have faith in the future of the markets, and continue to make well-reasoned investment decisions not based on chance or emotion. That's how investors win over the long term.

Chapter Ten

YOU'VE GOT TO HAVE FAITH

We've got to have faith if we want to create success for ourselves in the future. As the philosopher Charles Handy wrote in *The Empty Raincoat: Making Sense of the Future*, "We need to have faith in the future to make sense of the present."

It's a theme touched upon by many great men and women over the years. President John F. Kennedy said, "We can have faith in the future only if we have faith in ourselves." Martin Luther King Jr. put it this way: "Faith is taking the first step even when you don't see the whole staircase."

Whenever people ask us what we think the market's going to do next week, or next month, or next year, we always use that famous quote by J.P. Morgan: "It's going to fluctuate." But predicting the market is the exact opposite of predicting the weather. If someone asked you right now what the weather is going to be in thirty minutes, you could look out the nearest window and give them a pretty good guess.

"There are clear skies out there. It's calm. Humidity is low. The temperature is seventy-four degrees. Therefore, I predict that it's going to be around seventy-four degrees, with clear skies and low humidity, in thirty minutes."

However, if someone asked you what the weather is going to be like in thirty *years*, then you'd have no real way to answer. You could research the statistical averages for your location at this time of the year and make a prediction that is somewhere within that range, but there's no way to be sure. There's simply no way to predict the weather that far into the future.

Predicting what the markets will do is exactly the opposite. When you look back in history, you can see that the stock market in particular has always been volatile, with periods of ups and downs, but over the long term, it generally reverts to its average growth. Conversely, if you asked us what the market will do thirty minutes from now, we couldn't tell you. Anything could happen to the markets in the next thirty minutes. We've seen the market drop 1 percent in a couple of minutes right in the middle of the day, then bounce back up by the end of the day.

All it takes is some scary news report. Once, it was a false report about a bomb going off at the White House. As soon as it hit the news, the market reacted sharply, but then the report was revealed to be a hoax, and the market rebounded. For that reason, we couldn't tell you with any degree of certainty what the markets will do in thirty minutes, or in a few hours, or in a couple of days.

On the other hand, if you ask us where the market will be in thirty years, we could give you an answer with a reasonable amount of confidence. Why? Because every thirty-year period in the stock market has produced a return, and that growth has been, on average, fairly consistent. Indeed, this consistent growth is the main reason we invest, and it's the reason why we focus on *long-term* investments.

We don't buy stocks so we can sell them next week at a profit. We buy them so we can hold on to them for years, trusting that the market will continue to grow over the long run as it always has. You can have faith in the long-term performance of the stock market because that consistent growth over time, even in the face of sporadic downturns, is an essential part of the history of the stock market—indeed, the history of our entire economic system.

BELIEVE IN THE FUTURE

The predictability of the markets over long periods of time is the very reason why financial planning works. You can build a plan and have faith that it will work out because the *long-term* performance of the markets has been reliable, and there's every reason to believe it will continue to be reliable.

Why is this the case? How can we be confident that the markets will continue to grow over the long term as they have always done? First, because constant innovation and improvements in every industry lead toward economic growth. Second, the population of the world is constantly increasing, and more people allow for a larger economy. Third, inflation is built into our global monetary system, as we mentioned in a previous chapter, and that inflation tends to be reflected in the markets over time.

All three of these causes work together to create a consistent, long-term upward trend in the markets, and there's every reason to believe that they will continue to do so. The one thing that all financially successful people have in common is an unwavering faith in that long-term growth of the markets.

Warren Buffett is over ninety years old now, and he still talks constantly about where the market is going to be in thirty or forty years with optimism. Like other successful investors, he's been able to ignore the noise and tension that throws people off track. He's kept his eyes on the prize through difficult periods with unwavering confidence, and as a result, he's achieved some amazing long-term results.

If you're not confident that the long-term economy is going to grow and the markets are going to rise, then what's the point of investing at all? Think about it. When we invest, we're forgoing immediate gratification for the potential of having more money in the future to meet long-term goals, but if you don't believe that there's going to be expansion and growth, then you shouldn't be investing in the first place. It's not something you believe in, and you're likely to make unpredictable short-term decisions.

There's every reason for optimism. Historically, we can look back and see progress all the way back to the dawn of civilization.

Even before recorded history, people were learning, innovating, and progressing. The nomadic tribes eventually figured out that they could settle in one place, grow their own crops, and domesticate certain animals. Nomadic people became agricultural people, and settlements flourished. Settlements became cities.

Of course, sometimes those early societies grew beyond their capacity to feed their people, and they entered the early version of a recession. Suddenly, people were struggling, some were starving, and the city would suffer as a result, but eventually, civilization as a whole has always recovered and economic activity resumed.

That's how human civilization has developed for thousands of years. Cities rose and fell, cultures rose and fell, but human civilization across the board has trended toward progress in almost every area over the long term. That is the overarching story of humanity: an upward trend toward progress pockmarked with occasional setbacks caused by famine, natural disaster, disease, and war.

While there have been regional exceptions, on a global scale, human civilization has recovered from every downturn and progressed beyond it. The population has recovered from every decline and continued to grow. The macroscopic trend has been growth and advancement for all of human history.

There's no guarantee that this growth trend will continue indefinitely into the future, but we've never seen it *not* happen at any point in human civilization. Broadly, we see a trend toward human growth, progress, and development as far back as we can look. Furthermore, in many ways, we're alive at quite possibly the best time and place in history. Even if there are some significant problems, objectively speaking, we're in a time and place of great technological innovation and economic opportunity.

We've come through some dramatic market downturns, but the market is significantly bigger than it's ever been. Within the last few decades, we've seen the stock market cut in half twice—first from 2000 to 2003, then from 2007 to 2009. We saw the market drop by 34 percent from February 19 to March 23 of 2020. Every single one of these declines caused widespread fears, but in the end, every single one of them presented a tremendous buying opportunity.

In fact, they represent some of the best buying opportunities in history. People who bought into the market in 2008 and held on reaped incredible benefits when the market recovered and grew again. But people who were short-sighted, who responded emotionally to the dramatic downturn, missed out.

Let us be crystal clear on this point because it is incredibly important: every market downturn has proven to be a tremendous long-term buying opportunity!

Maybe you've seen the 2011 movie *Margin Call*, which tells the story of a Wall Street investment bank during the early stages of the 2008 financial crisis. Toward the end of the movie, Jeremy Irons's character, the CEO of the financial firm, gives a speech in which he lists a bunch of years in which financial crises took place. Here's what he says:

"It's certainly no different today than it's ever been. 1637, 1797, 1819, '37, '57, '84, 1901, '07, '29, 1937, 1974, 1987...and whatever we want to call this. It's all just the same thing over and over; we can't help ourselves. And you and I can't control it, or stop it, or even slow it. Or even ever-so-slightly alter it. We just react. And we make a lot of money if we get it right. And we get left by the side of the road if we get it wrong."

The movie is a cynical take, but he makes a compelling point. We can go back in time and see numerous massive declines. In 1637, the downturn was the result of a speculative bubble caused by the rising price of tulips from the Dutch Republic. In 1797, a land speculation bubble in the fledgling United States burst and caused a series of downturns. Panics, crises, downturns—they've happened time and time again, and we have recovered every single time.

Not long ago, Alex was invited to speak to about a hundred people at an engagement, and coincidentally, the S&P 500 had just closed at its highest point to date. He asked the attendees, "Which of you has ever lost money in the stock market?"

Every single hand in the room went up.

"How is that possible?" Alex asked. "The market is literally at the highest point it has *ever been* in history! If you bought stock at any point in your life—at any point in the history of the United States—before today, you've made money. Yet every single person in this room has raised their hand. How is that possible?"

The answer, of course, is that every person in that room had made an emotional decision about their investments at some point during a downturn and missed out on the growth when it recovered. They lacked faith in the market. At some point, they didn't trust that it would rebalance.

Of course, we all lose a little bit here and there when the market goes through an adjustment, but if you're a long-term investor with faith in the future, then you should *never* have a big loss on your books from investing (unless you unwisely invest an inordinate amount of money in the next Enron). Yes, there are going to be periods when the market is down, and the notional value of a stock is lower than you paid for it, but that's both normal and temporary!

We went through one of the most rapid declines of the last twenty years during early 2020, and people panicked. We found ourselves constantly telling clients, "The COVID pandemic is serious, and the market is reacting to it. Have faith that we will come through this. Recovery may take a couple of years, and we don't know when it will start or how fast it will happen. But the market *will* recover!"

We could say that with confidence because it always has. Thankfully, the recovery was extremely fast. We bounced right back and closed the year positive. At the time of this writing, the market has doubled from its value at the lowest point during 2020. People who lacked faith and sold all of their investments in 2020 were unable to get back in at the same place.

OPTIMISM ON THE ROAD TO SUCCESS

When you build a long-term financial plan, it's important to have faith and maintain optimism about the future. The markets will almost certainly do what they've always done: recover from downturns and continue to grow. Hold fast to that belief and don't let outside influences derail your plans.

If you have a long-time horizon in your retirement plans, if you don't need to access the money you're investing for twenty or thirty years, then you've got plenty of time to wait out any downturn. Our single best piece of advice to you is to invest as much money as you can possibly tolerate, as aggressively as you can, and keep it there. Just keep it there! If you can handle it, don't even open your financial statements.

We spoke to a man recently who told us, "I've been putting money into my 401(k) and investing in a prefabricated growth portfolio. I don't even look at the financial statements. I just shred them."

"Do you have any idea how much is in your investments?" we asked.

"Honestly, I have no idea," he replied.

Now, we're not actually recommending that you never look at your financial statements. It's tongue-in-cheek advice—you should know what your money is doing—but that's the power of having faith in what the market will do.

You know what erodes that faith? Seeing the market drop 34 percent in twenty-three trading days. If you get too emotionally wrapped up in the short-term performance of the market, then you're liable to make emotional decisions that can hinder or harm your long-term financial plan. So, our best advice is this: don't pay close attention to the day-to-day performance of the markets. Be optimistic, keep the faith, and hang in there. Let the markets do what they have always done: grow.

Chapter Eleven

BEWARE THE FINANCIAL MEDIA

The phrase, "If it bleeds, it leads," was first used by Eric Pooley in an article called "Grins, Gore, and Videotape" published in *New York* magazine in 1989 to describe the unofficial motto of television journalism. It was true then, and it's true now, though it's not limited to television journalism, by any means. In fact, online news outlets are desperately chasing ratings these days as much as anyone—and the financial media are guilty.

What drives ratings and page views? Emotion! The more emotion a news outlet can create with their reports and stories, the better the ratings are going to be. Thanks to risk aversion, stories about financial loss are always going to hit twice as hard as stories about financial gain, which means better ratings and more page views. That's why the financial media give so much time to analysts, economists, and investors predicting doom and gloom.

When the market gets a bit choppy, they don't bring financial advisors on the air to say, "Hey, stick with your game plan. Ride it out. The market's coming back." Even though this has generally been sound advice, it doesn't drive more viewers. What drives more viewers is fear.

The problem is, if you feed yourself on a steady diet of fear-driven financial media, it's going to erode your long-term optimism and produce excessive agita that can lead you to make a big investment mistake. So many investors missed out on growth in 2020 when the market dropped because the financial media got them scared. All the market has to do is turn slightly negative, and suddenly the financial media pundits are putting us in crisis mode.

Understand the impact that constant sensationalist doom-and-gloom reporting has on your financial decision-making. Guard yourself against it. Simple historical statistics can help. From

1991 to 2020, the daily fluctuation of the S&P 500 averaged 0.73 percent.[4]

Despite this, we've seen the market drop 0.7 percent, and the financial media run headlines that say things like, "Markets Plunge! Markets in Free Fall!" They'll show a trader on the floor with his head in his hands, lamenting that he just lost his kid's college fund, or he's not going to be able to pay his mortgage. This kind of sensationalism happens *every single time* there's a downturn in the market, even when it's within the daily statistical average!

When the markets are *really* volatile, that's when you need to stay optimistic more than ever, but that's also when the media go wild with negativity. We're all susceptible to this kind of sensationalism. Test yourself. Which of these headlines piques your interest more: "Modest Growth Expected in the Future," or "The Sky Is Falling! Markets Might Collapse!" Which article are you more likely to read?

You can't avoid negative reporting. It's everywhere. Every financial news outlet brings wild-eyed commentators on the air to

---

[4] Stats provided by FactSet.

rant about the end of the world. We've seen it time and time again over the years.

"The markets are going to drop hard," they'll say. "It's coming! The next great recession!"

Are they ever right? Well, even a broken clock is right twice a day. So, when the pundit who constantly predicts doom and gloom finally gets it right, he can boast, "See? I told you it was going to happen, and it happened! From now on, listen to me."

The reality is, nobody knows what the markets are going to do in the short term. Nobody. But, as we've said, we can be reasonably confident about what they are going to do in the long term, so that's where we should focus our attention. Unfortunately, even if 98 percent of financial experts agree on the long-term growth of the markets, there are always going to be a few oddballs with wild ideas about a financial apocalypse, and they're the ones who get air time.

The problem with economics is that you can spin your opinion using some elements of real data. It's not hard to take the same collection of numbers and use them to defend a whole range of predictions and opinions. Be aware of this.

THE COLOR OF A PREDATOR'S MOUTH

Understand the psychological games that are played for ratings. Even the colors that are used in graphics are intended to have an emotional impact. Red is typically used in graphics to depict a falling market, while green is used for a rising market.

Why is that? Ask any interior designer, and they'll tell you green is a calming color. A light shade of green is perfect for bedroom walls. Red is the color of passion and emotion. Evolution has predisposed us to fear the color red because it represents things like fire, blood, the inside of a predator's mouth.

Back during the financial crisis of 2008, we found ourselves watching market reports throughout the day. There were red arrows all over the place! Finally, we tried a little experiment where we reversed the colors on our screen so the falling market graphics were bright green. On that particular day, the market had dropped 3 percent, but we noticed that the bright green graphics showing the decline hit a lot softer.

Some online platforms for tracking your investment portfolio offer colors other than red and green, such as yellow and blue, to represent market declines and rises. Try it. You'll feel the difference.

Now, to be clear, we're not saying the media are the enemy. They're not trying to destroy you with their sensationalism and psychological tricks, but it's not their job to simply report facts. It's their job to sell advertising time and generate revenue, and that's what they're trying to do.

When we were growing up in the 1980s, viewers only had three or four choices for television news—NBC, ABC, CBS, and maybe Fox—along with a few newspapers. You could also get a little news on PBS and maybe on a religious program like *The 700 Club*. That was it.

These days, there are dozens of news channels to choose from, including Headline News, CNN, MSNBC, Bloomberg, CNBC, Fox News, and Fox Business. That's crazy enough, but online, there are literally *thousands* of websites where you can get your news and information, beginning with the blogs and message boards for each of the news channels. If you're really reckless, you can even get financial advice from places like Twitter or Reddit.

Thousands upon thousands of people are constantly disseminating editorialized commentary and ideas about the financial markets. The amount of information you have access to is mind-boggling, but each of these websites and channels still needs to generate ad revenue. This necessitates an even more bombastic approach to delivering the news.

Have you watched CNN lately? Pundits will be talking when all of a sudden music blares and a red banner flashes across the screen announcing "breaking news," and as a viewer, you think, "Uh oh, breaking news? What happened?" But the breaking news turns out to be another report from the same reporter talking about the same event that she's been talking about all day. Why is it presented so dramatically? To grab your attention and keep you watching until the next commercial break.

When it comes to the financial markets, the sensationalism is almost always pointed in the same direction: the stock market is going to crash. If an expert somewhere says a market correction is coming, somehow the "correction" is portrayed as a "crash."

"This expert suggests that a market crash is coming! How bad will it be? For that, we turn to our own resident expert."

Sometimes, it takes the form of wild predictions about which investments are good and which investments are bad. Guys like CNBC's Jim Cramer are entertaining, but their stock picks aren't better than anyone else's stock picks. It's fun to watch him ranting and leaping around the stage, but it's not his job to provide sound financial advice. It's his job to get ratings and drive ad revenue by putting on a good show.[5]

A PROFESSIONAL WHO KNOWS YOU

Recently, a client forwarded us an article from the website MarketWatch. While MarketWatch is generally a well-controlled news source, this particular article was an opinion piece filled with the same kind of alarmist nonsense that infests the rest of the financial media.

So, we responded to the client, "If you were seeking guidance for your own health, who would you go to?"

"A doctor, of course," he replied.

"You're half right," we said. "You wouldn't go to *a* doctor, you'd go to *your* doctor."

---

[5] There are multiple studies showcasing how Mr. Cramer's picks line up against the general market. Unsurprisingly, he doesn't stack up well. For an overview of the studies, see: Murray Coleman, "Jim Cramer vs. S&P 500: Chasing 'Mad Money,'" Index Fund Advisors, updated November 29, 2021, https://www.ifa.com/articles/cramer_chasing_mad_money/.

It's a subtle distinction, but an important one. If you have a sinus infection and you look online for the best treatment option, a medical website will probably tell you to take an antibiotic, but what if you're allergic to penicillin? What if your specific health situation isn't covered by the general information provided on medical websites?

That's why you go to your own doctor, a professional who knows your allergies, risk factors, and preferences, because he's far more likely to provide the solution that is best for you. A medical website might provide some accurate general information, but because of your specific situation, some of that general information might be dead wrong for you.

The same is true of financial websites. You can find plenty of financial advice online that is solid, but it may not be appropriate for you. For example, a client sent us an article about putting together a portfolio that recommended 60 percent large-cap US stocks, 30 percent small-cap US stocks, and 10 percent international stocks. The article claimed this is the optimal portfolio, and they presented a lot of back-tested data to prove it.

"It says this is the optimal portfolio," the client said. "Shouldn't I be allocating my investments like this?"

We told the client, "This is a very appropriate allocation for many people, but it's dead wrong for you. First, you've just retired, so you're already taking distributions from your assets. A portfolio that's this aggressive is way too volatile for the distributions you're currently taking. Your portfolio is designed to give you the best chance not to run out of money, but taking distributions at the wrong time from such an aggressive allocation could hurt you."

"Secondly," we added, "we've known you for ten years. When the markets get volatile, you get scared. That's a normal reaction. It's not wrong to feel anxious, but if you're too aggressive with your investments, then the first time the market corrects and drops 10 percent, and your $1 million portfolio loses $100,000 of notational value, you're going to panic. Your primal brain will desperately want to sell everything and move it all to cash."

"The way we've allocated your investments," we explained, "is designed to buffer you during down periods so you don't get sticker shock when you open your financial statement."

"That all makes sense to me," the client said. "So, what I read online is correct, but it's not right for me."

And that, beyond the ratings sensationalism, is the real point.

You can get information from financial media. Some of it will be good advice, but it can't be customized to your specific situations.

Asking us for medical advice is a bad idea. Getting medical advice from medical professionals online is better, but it's still not ideal. Only a personal physician will know enough about your specific health history and lifestyle to provide the best advice. The same goes for financial advice. If you're going to seek advice about your investment portfolio, 1) talk to a financial professional, and 2) work with someone who knows you and your situation. A respectable website or financial news outlet might provide you with some good general information, but that doesn't mean it's right for you.

IT HAPPENS TO EVERYONE

It happens to every professional investor out there. We see the markets become volatile, and we have an emotional reaction to it. That's why it's so important to understand how your investment plan is built, what it's accomplishing for you, and how it's designed to deal with volatility.

Periods of calm and periods of volatility are both inevitable. If you understand what your investment plan is doing for you, then you can maintain the correct balance throughout both good markets and bad.

Everything you do in life should be done purposefully. Don't approach the future with a scattershot approach. Clarify your desired outcome, develop a roadmap for reaching that desired outcome, and make the right choices to follow it.

That's true of every area of life, but it's certainly true of your financial planning. While you can't plan for every possible scenario, and trying to do so would be counterproductive, it's far worse not to plan for anything. The most successful people have a financial plan that is rational and reasonable; they have a game plan for achieving their goals.

We have a finite amount of time. The universe has been around thirteen billion years, and it'll almost certainly be around a lot longer. Physicists estimate that the heat death of the universe will not happen for many trillions of years. As humans, we get a hundred years if we're lucky, so plan well and make the most of it.

Chapter Twelve

YOU CAN'T TAKE IT WITH YOU

It's an old story that has been told thousands of times. Two men are attending the funeral of a local millionaire. As they stand beside his casket, gazing down at the nice suit adorning the body, one man turns to the other and says, "This guy was rich! I wonder how much he left behind."

And the second man replies, "Every cent!"

When it comes down to it, there are only two ways that a financial plan can fail. The first and most obvious way it can fail is if you run out of money. Most of the time, this happens when you don't plan or invest appropriately. The next thing you know, your retirement income has dried up and you're a seventy-five-year-old greeter at Walmart.

There's nothing wrong with being a seventy-five-year-old greeter if that's what you really want to do with your life. Go for it! But it's tragic to end up in a low-paying job when you should be enjoying your retirement years, simply because you didn't plan well.

The second way a financial plan can fail is if you die with plenty of money but a lot of regrets about the things you *didn't* do. Most of our clients have been good savers, and they invest well in accumulated assets. They also tend to have difficulty spending the money they've saved their whole adult lives, even though they saved and invested it specifically to use during their retirement years.

Sadly, we see too many older people with a lot of money *and* a lot of regrets about the things they wish they'd done. There's no sense in building income for your retirement if you're not going to use it to enjoy the life you've always dreamed of. Your financial plan is a living, breathing thing that needs to change as your situations and desires change. If it's too rigid and doesn't build some fun into your life, then you're going to end up regretting all the things you *wanted* to do, could *afford* to do, but *didn't* do.

And then you wind up lying in that casket like the guy in our opening story who left every cent of his money behind. You wind up with people at your funeral saying, "Wow, that person sure left a lot of money behind when they died. They didn't do a lot with it, though."

It's a shame.

Often, this unwillingness to spend money is driven by a fear that the money will run out. In reality, people should be just as scared of dying with way too much money, because that likely means they failed to do some things they wanted to do.

If you just want to spend your retirement living a simple life, that's fine. Do what makes you feel happy and comfortable. In that case, you might indeed wind up leaving a pretty big nest egg to your heirs, and there's nothing wrong with that. Knowing that you will be able to provide for your children or grandchildren might even give you some peace of mind that helps you enjoy your retirement years more. You're under no obligation to spend so much money that the first check you ever bounce is to the undertaker.

However, the goal of your retirement plan should be to live a fulfilling life. Back in the first chapter, we talked about the importance of figuring out what you really want out of life. That's the first step to a good financial plan. Once you're clear about what you want, then you can determine what your financial resources are capable of achieving for you. For example, maybe you discover that your retirement plan will be able to provide an income of $20,000 a month.

If a fulfilling life for you requires spending only $3,000 of that every month and leaving the rest to your heirs—if that's what makes you truly happy—then go for it. Your heirs (if you have them) might have to deal with estate taxes, but ultimately, they'll be able to do a lot with the money you've left them.

But we see far too many people being overly cautious out of fear. They're so nervous about spending the money they've acquired that they miss out on the retirement lifestyle they wanted to live. We can show them statistics and forward-looking projections that suggest their money is going to hold up just fine, but sometimes they just can't let go. They can't bring themselves to use the money, even on things they really want. What, then, was the point of all of that saving and investing?

THINK OF YOUR FINANCIAL LIFE IN PHASES

There are two primary phases to your financial life. First, there's the accumulation phase, when you're working, saving, investing, and letting your financial plan do its thing. Second, there's the distribution phase, which happens right around your retirement. This is when you start taking money out of what you've accumulated and spend it.

When you reach that second phase, your mindset has to change pretty dramatically. You've been faithful in setting money aside for years. You have savings that you haven't touched in decades. Now it's time to start spending that money, and you have to feel okay about it.

Years ago, Alex's mother shared with him one of her fundamental rules of personal finance, and it has stuck with him ever since. She said, "Spend only some of what you make, and none of what you save or invest." That's a great mindset for the accumulation phase. If you make $10,000 a month after taxes, and you spend $5,000 of it and put the rest away and never think about it, then you're going to build substantial wealth over the years.

Once you reach the second phase, it's time to transition from accumulation to distribution. Now, all of a sudden, you're no longer making money, except perhaps a bit from Social Security and maybe, if you're one of the lucky few, a pension. Somehow, you have to get comfortable with the idea of touching that big nest egg you've accumulated, the nest egg that you've told yourself for years not to touch.

This turns out to be quite a challenge for many people. Spending that money feels contrary to everything they've been taught for the last three or four decades, and they struggle to overcome that mental block.

MAKE THE MOST OF THE GO-GO YEARS

You can further subdivide your retirement years into three stages, which we'll call the *go-go* years, the *slow-go* years, and the *no-go* years. During the go-go years, you're still healthy and active, so you can do a lot of things. During the slow-go years, you're getting older, and you're starting to slow down. You're no longer as active. You don't take as many trips, and your desires are changing. Finally, in the no-go years, you're at a point in life where you just can't do much of anything. You're not that healthy, and you have very little energy.

The go-go years in the early part of your retirement are the best time for you to take advantage of your retirement and do all of the things you've always dreamed about. Unfortunately, these are the years when retirees are often struggling to shift their mindset from accumulating to spending. Their every instinct tells them not to touch the money, so they keep sitting on their nest egg as much as they possibly can.

By the time they get comfortable spending the money, they're entering the no-go stage, and they no longer have the health or energy to do much. This is when regret starts to hit people.

"Why didn't I take a trip to Paris? I always wanted to see Paris, and now I just can't travel that far!"

"Why didn't I buy an RV and travel across the country? My spouse and I always talked about doing that, and now I'm not healthy enough to drive."

Make it your goal to enter the no-go stage with no regrets regarding your finances. None of us are promised tomorrow, but we should still plan to live a long time. Create a financial plan for that very purpose. Be mindful of balancing your current satisfaction with your big dreams. You want to have enough income to support a long, healthy life, but don't miss out on your big dreams, if you can comfortably afford them.

So, how do you deal with the conflict in your mind as you make the transition from accumulation to distribution? Remember, as with other struggles in financial planning, the source of this conflict is rarely based on facts or statistics. Usually, it's purely an emotional response to fear—fear that something catastrophic is going to happen and all the money will disappear.

Unfortunately, there's no magic bullet that can make the anxiety suddenly and completely go away, but we find that the best way to overcome it is to develop a better understanding of where you actually stand financially and what capacity you truly have.

Of course, you have to make reasonable purchasing decisions once you reach the distribution phase of your financial life. It is entirely possible to hit retirement and then blow through your money way too fast. We've seen people do it. They've saved for decades, then they enter retirement and start spending to excess. Before they know it, the money's gone, and they've got years of life left to find some new income.

We take our role as financial educators very seriously, and about 80 percent of what we do is teach people the fundamentals of putting together a solid financial plan and investment strategy that will enable them to achieve their life goals. We always want to empower people to make the best decisions about their money on their own, so they don't need someone else to make those decisions for them. A big part of empowering them is simply helping them get through anxious times so they can stick with their plan, whether they are accumulating or distributing.

Ironically, the people who spend their accumulation years feeling a little nervous tend to do okay once they reach retirement. The ones who really struggle are often the ones who have never really worried about their financial plan until they approach the transition, because they haven't felt any compulsion to develop financial discipline or perseverance. So they start spending that money wildly on things they never wanted.

"Oh, I never owned a boat. Maybe I'll get a boat."

Without ever planning ahead of time, they pull $150,000 out of their retirement fund for a boat that they never identified as a financial goal when they made their plans. That reckless spending has an impact on the rest of your life's budget! Now there's a substantial reduction in your spending capacity for the next twenty-five to thirty years.

You have to understand the financial impact of big purchases during your retirement years. Plan for them in advance. Otherwise, you might inadvertently reduce your budget for the remainder of your retirement.

It's about finding the right balance between spending on the things you really want in life and creating enough income to live out the rest of your life. If you identify your goals well in advance, you're more likely to invest in a way that will help you comfortably afford them. Just don't let anxiety paralyze you so that you fail to realize the big goals you've set for yourself.

No, you don't want to be so cavalier that you spend $2 million from your retirement fund in the first two years. That money represents all of the hard work you've done over the years saving and investing. You didn't win the lottery; you practiced delayed gratification in order to make your retirement years more comfortable. So make sure the money is there for you.

Having said that, let us be clear: over-*saving* is a far more common problem than over-*spending* for people who have taken the time to practice good retirement planning. You begin the process of creating your financial plan by imagining the end result and clarifying the kind of lifestyle you want to experience during your retirement years. Take this exercise to the very end.

We opened this chapter with a funeral, so now envision your own funeral. Reflect on the person you will have become and all of the things you will have done. What sort of legacy do you want to leave behind? What do you want those final years to look like? Will you get to the end of your life regretting the things you never did?

Set your goals, work toward them diligently, and then, when you arrive at your retirement years, live the life you envisioned as much as your finances, health, and time allow. Adjust your mindset so you can begin spending all of that money you've worked hard to save. Make it your goal to reach your final years without regret and leave behind the legacy that you want. It's the best that any of us can do with the finite time we've been given.

CONCLUSION

By reading this book, it's our hope that you've been able to start thinking about money on your own terms. This is a topic we spend many, many hours each week thinking about and talking about with our clients. Our goal here has been to provide some of the most important lessons we've learned over the years, so you can live a fuller and more fulfilling financial life.

We've clarified what money is and what it can do for you. Remember, there are essentially only four things you can do with money: buy things, buy experiences, help others, or save it for future use. The purpose of good financial planning is to figure out the right proportions of those four things to enable you to be happy about the decisions you've made when you reach retirement and life's completion.

This is difficult to do unless you have a good understanding of how to put money aside, how to allocate it, how to avoid mistakes, and how to maintain a healthy mindset about investing. As you've read this book, maybe you've become more aware of some things you need to work on. Maybe you're not putting enough money away. Maybe you don't have a good budget. Maybe you've never clarified what you're working toward.

As we mentioned earlier, the old saying goes, "The best day to plant a tree was twenty years ago. The second-best day to do it is today." We can apply that same idea to financial planning. The best day to start putting together a budget, start saving, and start investing was some time in the past. The second-best day is today. Whether you're sixteen or fifty-five, five years from retirement or five years into retirement, start examining your own financial position now. It's never too early, and it's never too late, to start making good financial decisions.

Yes, the earlier you start making good decisions, the greater impact those decisions are going to make on your future. However, you can still make an impact, no matter how far along you are. Regret won't fix anything, so instead of looking back at all of the mistakes and poor financial decisions you've made in the past, start thinking about money in a better way today.

Just last week, we had a conversation with a young couple. The guy was in his midthirties, and he'd listened to our podcast. He called our office with some questions, and we invited him and his spouse in to chat. During our conversation, he said, "I'm already past thirty, and I just feel like I haven't done anything. I made a lot of bad financial choices, and I'm really behind the eight ball on my financial planning."

"You're still relatively young," we told him. "You have plenty of time to change your trajectory. Would you be in a better position financially if you'd made the right choices ten years ago? Of course. However, you still have decades to start making an impact on your retirement. If you plan to retire at sixty, you can start moving the needle in that direction today."

The same message applies to you, no matter how far along you are in your career or what bad decisions you've made in your past. Yes, it would have been better to start making the right decisions years ago, but you can't do anything about that. All you can do is start making the right decisions today. If you start goal-setting, saving, investing, and allocating your assets today, you will move the needle closer to where you want to be when you retire.

Remember what we said about going to a personal physician who really knows you? If you're in your twenties or thirties, it's the perfect time to start working with a good financial advisor, someone who will understand your specific vision, needs, and preferences. Of course, you can do this on your own as well. Just make sure you figure out how aggressively you can invest without endangering your own psychological well-being.

It's also a good idea to have a professional with investing expertise, so you put your money in the right places to achieve your long-term goals. We see people making all kinds of irrational investment decisions because they just don't know any better.

If you do decide to work with a financial advisor, look for someone who is a good fit. No advisor is right for everyone. At Birch Run Financial, we have a great team, and we're ready to help you with your long-term financial planning.

However, like most financial advisors, we're not "jacks-of-all-trades." We work better with some clients than others. Many financial advisors specialize in specific areas. For example, some work primarily with business owners. Some work with government employees. Others focus on corporations. Find the right individual or team to help you through the process of financial planning, and your results are going to be better.

It might sound strange to hear us say this, but if we're not the right financial advisors for you, that's perfectly fine. Find someone you're comfortable with because your financial future is too important. Make the most of your finite time, create the right path to financial freedom, and live a life without regrets.

ACKNOWLEDGMENTS

Writing a book is tough. We've done it before, and for some unknown reason, we chose to do it again. Without the friendship and support of so many, none of the words you've just read would have made it to the page. To properly express our gratitude would take up far more pages than you would likely care to read, so we'll keep it as brief as possible.

To our wives, Rachel and Patty, who have (and continue to) put up with our erratic schedules and stressful careers, we are grateful for your love and support. To our parents, Ed and Susie Lambert, and Kate Cabot, we are grateful for the financial lessons you taught us from a young age. We hope that we've made you proud. To our children, Avery and Elena Lambert, and Samantha and Jack Cabot, thank you for giving us a reason to work so hard. We hope to instill in you the lessons we've learned over the years. You make us smile, laugh, and sometimes scratch our heads in wonder. It's a joy to watch you grow.

To our team, Bernadette, Ian, Ryan, and Kayla, it is an honor and a privilege working alongside you each day. Our business thrives because of your hard work and dedication. Thank you for your support and loyalty over the years. To the team at Scribe Media, Frances Jane, Bianca, Beth and Jeff, thank you for making the process of writing this book so much smoother than the last. If we ever forget how much work this was and decide to write another, you're the first people we'll call.

A special thanks to Jeff at Scribe Media. It was an absolute pleasure to work with you on so many conference calls. And thank you for putting up with Alex's rambling, nonsensical stories. You are a more patient man than most.

We are deeply grateful to our clients, without whom none of this would be possible. The trust that you place in our team is something we do not take lightly, and each day we strive to become better at what we do. For those clients who took the leap of faith back in 2012 when we started our company, we are especially grateful. Your support and encouragement kept us afloat during an unimaginably stressful time in our lives.

And to our readers, thank you for taking the time to read *Mastering the Money Mind*. If you are able to gain even a marginally better understanding of your personal finances as a result of this book, we have done our jobs. The journey to financial independence is a long and meandering path. If you'd like a little guidance along the way, give us a call. We're happy to walk beside you.

CONTACT INFORMATION

Birch Run Financial LLC

595 E Swedesford Rd Ste 360

Wayne, PA 19087

484-395-2190

info@birchrunfinancial.com

Securities offered through Raymond James Financial Services, Inc., member FINRA/SIPC. Investment advisory services offered through Raymond James Financial Services Advisors, Inc. Birch Run Financial is not a registered broker/dealer, and is independent of Raymond James Financial Services.

ABOUT THE AUTHORS

ED LAMBERT

Ed is a managing partner and co-founder of Birch Run Financial. He earned a bachelor's degree in economics from Ursinus College in Collegeville, Pennsylvania, and earned the CRPC® designation from the College for Financial Planning®. He began his career in the capital markets division of Morgan Stanley in 2001 and holds Series 7 and 66 securities licenses. He has been featured in numerous publications, including *The Philadelphia Inquirer* and *Philadelphia Business Journal*, and has appeared on NBC 10 News in Philadelphia as a retirement planning commentator.

As a Chartered Retirement Planning Counselor, Ed has in-depth knowledge of the needs individuals face both before and after retirement, and engages in retirement planning for a variety of important issues, such as sources of retirement income, employer-sponsored retirement plans, tax planning, retirement cash flow, asset management, estate planning, and more. Ed lives in Newtown Square with his wife, Rachel, and daughters, Avery and Elena. He spends much of his free time in Ocean City, New Jersey, where you'll often find him fishing on the beach in the early morning hours.

ALEX CABOT

Alex is a managing partner and co-founder of Birch Run Financial and has been working directly with Ed Lambert since 2008. Alex graduated with honors from Washington University in St. Louis, earning a degree in physics and classical studies. He earned the ChFC® designation from the American College, a nonprofit educator with the highest level of academic accreditation. As a Chartered Financial Consultant®, Alex has completed one of the most extensive educational programs on all aspects of financial planning, adheres to strict ethical standards, and is committed to continuing education.

He holds Series 6, 7, 9, 10, 63, and 65 licenses. He has been quoted in *The Wall Street Journal* and is a regular guest on NBC 10 News in Philadelphia. Along with Ed, he has spoken to students at Ursinus College on a number of occasions. In

2018, Alex was honored by *Forbes* magazine as a "Top Next Gen Financial Advisor." In his free time, Alex enjoys spending time with his wife, Patty, and children, Jack and Samantha. He is active in charitable endeavors with the Shriners Hospital for Children and is an avid cyclist and chess player.

ABOUT *FORBES* RANKINGS

The *Forbes* ranking of Best-In-State Wealth Advisors, developed by SHOOK Research, is based on an algorithm of qualitative criteria, mostly gained through telephone and in-person due diligence interviews, and quantitative data. Those advisors that are considered have a minimum of seven years' experience, and the algorithm weights factors like revenue trends, assets under management, compliance records, industry experience and those that encompass best practices in their practices and approach to working with clients. Out of approximately 32,725 nominations received, based on thresholds, more than 5,000 advisors received the award. Portfolio performance is not a criteria due to varying client objectives and lack of audited data. Neither *Forbes* nor SHOOK receives a fee in exchange for rankings. This ranking is not indicative of an advisor's future performance, is not an endorsement, and may not be representative of an individual client's experience. Neither Raymond

James nor any of its financial advisors or RIA firms pay a fee in exchange for this award/rating. Raymond James is not affiliated with *Forbes* or Shook Research, LLC. For more information: SHOOKresearch.com.

CPSIA information can be obtained
at www.ICGtesting.com
Printed in the USA
BVHW050946080522
636253BV00006B/14/J